ALSO BY JIMMY BRESLIN

FICTION

The Gang That Couldn't Shoot Straight
World Without End, Amen
.44 (with Dick Schaap)
Forsaking All Others
Table Money
He Got Hungry and Forgot His Manners
I Don't Want to Go to Jail: A Good Novel

NON-FICTION

Sunny Jim: The Life of America's Most Beloved Horseman, James Fitzsimmons
Can't Anybody Here Play This Game?
The World of Jimmy Breslin
How the Good Guys Finally Won
The World According to Breslin
Damon Runyon: A Life
I Want to Thank My Brain for Remembering Me
The Short Sweet Dream of Eduardo Gutiérrez
The Church That Forgot Christ

THE MAFIA RAT

A TRUE STORY

JIMMY BRESLIN

MAINSTREAM
PUBLISHING

EDINBURGH AND LONDON

This edition, 2009

First published in United States of America in 2008 by
HarperCollins Publishers
10 East 53rd Street, New York, NY 10022

First published in Great Britain in 2008 by
MAINSTREAM PUBLISHING COMPANY
(EDINBURGH) LTD
7 Albany Street
Edinburgh EH1 3UG

ISBN 9781845964801

A catalogue record for this book is available
from the British Library

Typeset in Caslon and Century Gothic

CP

FOR SHEILA SMITH

NOTABLE APPEARANCES

FEDERAL COURT JUDGE JACK B. WEINSTEIN, a master of his trade.

BURTON KAPLAN, the witness. Read and remember him.

LOU EPPOLITO, one of the cops Kaplan happened to mention.

STEPHEN CARACAPPA, also drew some discussion.

ANTHONY 'GASPIPE' CASSO, described as a homicidal maniac. Beyond that, he has a bad reputation.

MITRA HORMOZI, ROBERT HENOCH, Assistant US Attorneys.

BRUCE CUTLER, EDWARD HAYES, BETTINA SCHEIN, defence attorneys.

JUDGE DEBORAH KAPLAN, Burt's daughter. A New York State Supreme Court judge.

THE INCARCERATED

They are proof that the Mafia is law-abiding. They always go to prison.

JOE MASSINO

GEORGE ZAPPOLA

CHRISTY 'TICK' FURNARI

TONY CAFÉ

PETER GOTTI

SAMMY GRAVANO

THE DECEASED

ANNETTE DIBIASE

ISRAEL GREENWALD

JOHN OTTO HEIDEL

JAMES BISHOP

MIKE SALERNO

EDDIE LINO

GOOD NICKY GUIDO

JAMES HYDELL

JAMES HYDELL'S DOG

JOEY GALLO

JOEY GALLO'S LION

LARRY GALLO

BIG MAMA GALLO

PAUL CASTELLANO

JOHN GOTTI

FRANK SANTORA

ANTHONY DILAPI

BRUNO FACCIOLA

JIMMY 'THE CLAM' EPPOLITO

JIM-JIM, HIS SON

ALIVE AND FREE AS OF THIS WRITING

SAL REALE

BAD NICKY GUIDO

PROLOGUE

What I'm doing, I'm kissing the mirror, and I'm doing it so I can see myself kissing and get it exactly right, no tongue and no fucking slop. This way I can go into the clubhouse and kiss them on the cheeks the way I'm supposed to. That's the Mafia. We kiss hello. We don't shake hands. We kiss.

I am at the mirror because I'm afraid of lousing up on kissing. When you kiss a guy and he gives you a kiss back, you make sure that your kissing comes across as Mafia, not faggot. That's why I'm practising in front of the mirror.

This is real Mafia. For years, cops and newspaper reporters glorified the swearing-in ceremony with the needle and the holy picture in flames and the old guy asking the new guy questions, like they all knew so much. The whole thing added up to zero. The kissing is different. It comes from strength and meaning. If you kiss, it is a real sign that you're in the outfit. You see a man at the bar, you kiss him. You meet people anyplace, you kiss them. Like a man. It doesn't matter who sees you. They're supposed to see.

It all started when John 'Sonny' Franzese and Joey Brancato, both big guys in the Colombo outfit, bumped into each other one day on the corner of Lorimer Street and Metropolitan Avenue in Greenpoint, which is in Brooklyn, and they kissed each other on the cheeks. The only thing anybody on Metropolitan Avenue knew was that they had never seen it done before. The moment the men kissed, it became a street rule. This was at least fifty years ago. Immediately they were doing it on 101st Avenue in Ozone Park and Cross Bay Boulevard in Howard Beach. Soon even legitimate citizens were doing it.

Sonny Franzese was born in Italy, brought here by his family when he was two. The family settled on Lorimer Street, which is made of two-storey frame houses, home built, and a bakery and restaurant. At a young age, Sonny failed to behave. In school, he also fell short. Even in the army for a brief time, he received a poor report card. He sparkled on local police reports, and his name got stars on FBI sheets.

The feds soon realised all they had to do was follow guys who kiss each other and they'd know the whole Mafia. Still nobody stopped.

Some guys said that Sonny Franzese had nothing to do with it. 'Italian men always kiss,' they claimed. But my friend Anthony – Tony Café – who is the boss of Metropolitan Avenue, says that when Sonny Franzese and Joey Brancato kissed it was the start of a great way for tough guys to know each other. It's like a password, only it's more personal.

The only thing anybody can agree on is the clout the old Black Hand had for a while. It came from the smallest villages in Sicily, where people in need of a favour or a goat went to the village priest for help. They would kiss his hand. Over the centuries, Sicily was raided and raped by many other countries. They raided and raped and afterward went into blacksmith shops and stuck their hands into cans of black paint, then slapped the walls outside to frighten anybody who passed. The Sicilians soon took over and began sending extortion notes decorated with black hands and demands for money from the immigrants crowding into downtown New York: 'Pay or Die'. Many paid.

The thing worked for a long time. Maybe we are talking about 1960, when I was in the village of Lercara Friddi, in the hills outside of Palermo, on a day of frigid rain. I was in the vestibule of the local church, large and leaky and falling down. I asked a man for the name of the church, and he said, 'Church? This is a cathedral.'

Outside in the narrow alley was a cow. The street of low stone houses ended at a field where narrow-gauge rail tracks led into a deserted sulphur mine. Kids in short pants and bare legs huddled in doorways and played cards.

The next morning, on the way to the airport, I found an Italian–English dictionary that I used to buy a stamp pad. I got a handful of postcards and stood off to the side of the ticket counter and smacked my hand on the ink pad and then on one of the postcards. I did this several times. The ticket clerk, pretty and bright as you want, walked over frowning.

'I need you,' I said. 'I want to write a thing in Italian.'

'What?'

'Put down "Pay or Die" in Italian.'

She sighed. 'Do you really want such silliness?'

I told her sure, that's what I want, and she made a face and told me again how silly it was. Then she told me to put down '*Paghi o Mori*'.

She said, 'That is the Sicilian.'

I took those cards and put stamps on them and mailed them to several people I knew back home in New York. The postcards fell on Queens in an attack so sudden and surprising that people's legs gave out as they read. Dr Philip Lambert, a dentist who ran a fixed dice game in his waiting room on Jamaica Avenue, was shaking as he showed the card to the veteran cheat Nicky the Snake.

'Look at this,' the Snake said, 'it's from Palermo. Doc, it's real. What did you do to them? Nobody here is heavy enough to make them go away.'

The doc tried. He took the postcard to Joe Massino of the Bonanno mob. Joe looked at it and frowned.

'One guy can help you,' he said. 'God.'

From then on, Doc Lambert lived a life of noisy desperation. He went to the Queens travel agency favoured by Sicilians and got people to carry notes to Palermo and give them to taxi drivers. The notes begged the Black Hand to let him live. This made him different from the others who received postcards and writhed in silent fear. When a mobster from the neighbourhood was killed, the postcard holders believed the Black Hand had struck. Doc Lambert took nervous breaths as he drilled teeth and hoped that he didn't slip and go through the guy's tongue. He also hoped to go on living. As far as I know, he died of natural causes.

ONE

UNITED STATES DISTRICT COURT
EASTERN DISTRICT OF NEW YORK
US Courthouse
Brooklyn, New York
March 14, 2006
10.00 A.M.

CR-05-0192

UNITED STATES OF AMERICA
v.
STEPHEN CARACAPPA and
LOUIS EPPOLITO
Defendants

BEFORE THE HONOURABLE JACK B. WEINSTEIN
UNITED STATES DISTRICT JUDGE and a jury.

APPEARANCES:
For the Government:
ROSLYNN R. MAUSKOPF
US Attorney
By: ROBERT HENOCH
MITRA HORMOZI
DANIEL WENNER

Assistant US Attorneys
One Pierrepont Plaza
Brooklyn, New York 11201

For the Defendants:
EDWARD WALTER HAYES, ESQ.
RAE DOWNES KOSHETZ, ESQ.
For Defendant Caracappa
BRUCE CUTLER, ESQ.
BETTINA SCHEIN, ESQ.
For Defendant Eppolito
(Open court-case called.)

THE COURT: Good morning everyone. Sit down, please.

THE UNITED STATES CALLS BURTON KAPLAN.

THE CLERK: Stand and raise your right hand. Do you swear or affirm to tell the truth, the whole truth and nothing but the truth under penalty of perjury?

THE WITNESS: I do.

THE CLERK: Your full name, sir.

THE WITNESS: Burton Kaplan.

DIRECT EXAMINATION OF KAPLAN BY ASSISTANT US ATTORNEY HENOCH.

Q: How old are you, sir?

A: Seventy-two.

Q: Are you currently incarcerated?

A: Yes.

Q: Sir, I would like to ask you to look around the courtroom, specifically at this table, and tell the jury if there is anybody sitting there that you recognise.

A: Yes.

Q: Can you tell the jury who you recognise?

A: Louis Eppolito and Stephen Caracappa.

Q: Can you please for the record point out an article of clothing that Mr Eppolito is wearing?

A: Grey suit with a light tie.

Q: What about Mr Caracappa?

A: Dark suit.

Q: Did you have a business relationship with Mr Eppolito and Mr Caracappa?

A: Yes.

Q: Can you please tell the jury what the nature of that business relationship was?

A: They were detectives on the New York Police Department who brought me information about wiretaps, phone taps, informants, ongoing investigations and imminent arrests and murders. They did murders and kidnapping for us.

Q: What did you do for them in exchange for this?

A: I paid them.

He cannot believe that he is doing this: that he is sitting on a witness stand to tell of a life of depravity without end. Burton Kaplan looks like a businessman in the noon swarm of Manhattan's garment centre: an old man with a high forehead and glasses, in a dark suit and white shirt. His face and voice show no emotion, other than a few instances of irritation when one of the lawyers asks something he knows and they do not. 'You are wrong, Counsellor,' he snaps. His eyes seem to blink a lot, but his words do not.

'Are you a member of the Mafia?' he is asked.

'No, I can't be a member. I'm Jewish.'

Jerry Shargel, Kaplan's lawyer for years, says, 'Bertie looks like a guy who is standing outside his temple waiting for an aliyah.' An honorary role in the service.

Kaplan's face has no lines of the moment, the voice is bare of emotion, with no modulation, as if a carpenter makes level each sentence. He does not differentiate between telling of a daughter's wedding reception and of an attempt to bury a body in ground frozen white in a Connecticut winter. It was bad enough that he had to drive alone with the body in the trunk and on a night so frigid that he shook with the cold. He finally tossed the body through the ice and into the nearest river.

Burton Kaplan brought that ice into the courtroom. Right away I see this old ice house on the corner of 101st Avenue in Ozone Park. The guy on the platform pulls the burlap cover from a frozen block and with an ice pick scratches the outline of the fifteen-cent piece I am there to get. He stabs the ice and first there is a crack that looks like a small wave and then the block explodes into white. One tug and the fifteen-cent piece goes on your shoulder for carrying to the icebox on the back porch. And now I have a name for Kaplan: 'Icebox.'

This suggests that he has bodies on hooks in a freezer somewhere. Close enough. Ask Burt Kaplan a question on the stand and he draws an outline in the ice, and then he answers and there is the explosion. The fifteen-cent piece separates from the block, and Burt Kaplan comes out of the cold with stories that kill. Yes, they did murder Eddie Lino. Caracappa did the firing. Yes, poor young honest Nicky Guido got killed by mistake. Gaspipe Casso wouldn't pay any extra money to find the right guy. Kaplan has a morgue full of answers.

He does not come out of a hovel where tough guys, as they are called, are raised three and four in one bed in a wretched family and dinner is anything stolen. He was raised on Vanderbilt Avenue in Brooklyn, a street of neat two- and three-storey attached houses with stores on the first floor. Everybody had a job. Kaplan's father was an electrician. The family had an appliance store and a liquor store. He went to one of the best public high schools in North America, Brooklyn Technical, and, in what often seemed to be the story of his life, he stayed there for a year and a half and was so close to legitimate success when he quit. Of Brooklyn Tech, he laments, 'I wish I stood there.'

Instead, he was a great merchant, too great, and after he sold everything that did belong to him, he sold things that did not. As there were no thrills in constant legitimacy, he loved thievery. This resulted in him moving up from Vanderbilt Avenue at age thirty-nine to Lewisburg Penitentiary on his first sentence, four years, federal.

Today, at seventy-two, he still owes eighteen years to the penitentiary on drug charges, and he is in court to talk his way out of them.

We are in a room that is the setting for what is supposed to be the first great mob trial of the century, that of the murderous Mafia Cops, Louis Eppolito and Stephen Caracappa. They were detectives in Brooklyn who sold confidential information and murdered for the Mafia. Burton Kaplan was their handler for the Lucchese organised-crime family.

I was hesitant about this trial from the start. These criminals held their secret meetings at a bar next to a golf course. If you look at how mobsters live today, you would say middle class and be right. The late, great Queens defence attorney Klein the Lawyer once said on behalf of some beast, 'How could he commit a crime? He lives in a house.' Middle class drowns excitement wherever you run into it. And the idea of cops who use their badges to murder depresses me. It is dreary and charmless and lacks finesse. It promises no opportunity to marvel, much less laugh.

I am at an early hearing when the defendants come into the courtroom: Eppolito fat and sad eyed, Caracappa a thin, listless nobody. I stare at my hands. Am I going to write seventy thousand words about these two? Rather I lay brick.

Then the trial starts, and I am pulled out of my gloom. An unknown

name on the prosecution witness list, an old drug peddler, a lifelong
fence, steals the show and turns the proceeding into something that
thrills: the autobiography of Burton Kaplan, criminal. Right away I
think, Fuck these cops. I have found my book.

TWO

DIRECT EXAMINATION OF BURTON KAPLAN BY ASSISTANT US ATTORNEY HENOCH.

Q: Who is shown in those photographs?

A: Tommy Galpine and myself. Number A was in my house. Number B I believe is Bonaparte's Restaurant when my wife and I were godparents for his kid, for his oldest boy.

Q: When did you meet him?

A: I met him when I came out of Lewisburg. He was sixteen.

Q: How old were you?

A: Probably forty. He worked for Ciro Sales. He worked in their warehouse loading trucks. I was doing my air-conditioning installations.

Q: Did you also do illegal things together?

A: Tommy sold some cocaine that I had – that I shared in the profits. We were – he worked for Ray Fontaine in the marijuana business, and when Ray Fontaine was missing, Tommy became my partner in the marijuana business.

Q: Tell us the other types of crimes you committed, Mr Kaplan.

A: Kidnapping, money laundering, obstruction of justice, murder. In 1981, I went to jail for conspiracy to manufacture Quaaludes. I got a habit of being arrested in my life.

I can barely handle legitimate people. They all proclaim immaculate honesty, but each day they commit the most serious of all felonies, being a bore. To whom do you care to listen: Warren Buffett, the second-richest and single most boring person on earth, or Burt Kaplan out of Bensonhurst, Brooklyn?

He testifies in simple declarative sentences: subject, verb and object, one following the other to start a rhythm that is compelling to the jury's ear. As I listen on this first morning of excruciating excitement, Kaplan comes out of all the ages of crime, out of Dostoyevsky, out of the Moors Murders, out of Murder Inc. A few words spoken by Burt Kaplan on his Brooklyn porch send animals rushing out to kill. I am thinking this when the court breaks for lunch. I go over to the Park Plaza Diner right across the street. When I walk in, Bettina Schein comes up to me. She is a pretty and smart criminal lawyer assisting Bruce Cutler, who represents one of the cops.

'What did you think of the witness?' she says.

'I was just thinking of—'

'Raskolnikov!' she says.

Q: Where were you born and raised?

A: Brooklyn, New York. I was born in Sheepshead Bay, and I moved to Vanderbilt Avenue, I guess it's the start of Bed-Stuy, when I was four, five. And I moved to Bensonhurst after I got married.

Q: Can you tell the jury what your father did for a living?

A: He was an electrician.

Q: Can you tell the jury the address of where you were raised?

A: 595 Vanderbilt Avenue. Between Bergen and Dean. It was an appliance store that was my family's – mine, my brother's and my mother's – before my brother got the liquor store.

Q: Can you tell the jury, are you married?

A: Forty-nine years. I have a daughter and one grandchild.

Q: Tell the jury about your educational background, sir.

A: I graduated high school, and then after I got out of the navy, I went to electronics school . . .

Q: Can you tell them a little more about your job in the navy?

A: I was doing copying codes, Russian codes, cryptography and crypton analysis. Most of the time I was in Japan. The last year that I was in the navy, I worked in Fort Meade, and I was offered a job with NSA.

Q: When you got out of the navy, what jobs have you held?

A: 1956, I went back into the appliance business. I was partners in a store with my brother and my mother. We sold appliances, and we installed them and repaired them. After that, I became incarcerated in Lewisburg Prison, and when I got out it was 1973 and I went to work for a company by the name of Ciro Sales, P.C. Richard, M and B Radio. I did all their installations of washing machines, dryers, air conditioners, dishwashers. In 1975, I went into the clothing business. When I was on Vanderbilt Avenue, with my brother and my mother, I did an air-conditioning job of a social club near my business, for a gentleman by the name of Charlie Parasella, and he introduced me to Jimmy Eppolito, who had a club on Grand Avenue called the Grand Mark. They played cards upstairs, and they asked me to go there and measure it for air-conditioning, and I did it, and he gave me the job, and I installed the air conditioners. There was somebody in Ciro's warehouse that asked me if I wanted to buy some air conditioners off of him, and I did.

Q: So what? That doesn't sound illegal.

A: No. It was Ciro's property, not the guy's in the warehouse.

Q: So they were stolen?

A: Yes, they definitely were stolen.

Before he continues with his résumé, we should note that the above-mentioned Jimmy 'the Clam' Eppolito, a well-known gangster, is the uncle of one of the Mafia Cops on trial here and thus provides his murderous nephew with a low-life pedigree. The uncle will come up again before we are through.

Q: Mr Kaplan, have you ever committed a crime in your life?

A: Yes. Most of my crimes in the early days was selling goods stolen from interstate shipment. The first time I went to – I went to prison for flashcubes. I received probation, and then I – I sold some pants from an interstate shipment and was sentenced to four years in Lewisburg Penitentiary. I was arrested for having hairdryers in my possession that were stolen, but the case was dismissed. In 1983, I was arrested for possible participation in a heroin conspiracy. It was dismissed because I wasn't involved in it.

In 1993, I was arrested in a conspiracy to sell stolen Peruvian passports. That was also dismissed, because we proved that we believed the passports were legal and that we were selling them in Hong Kong, and the selling of passports in Hong Kong to Chinese people was legal. I flew to China with my lawyer to prove it. The case was dismissed.

In – in 1981, I was, I went to jail for, I already said that.

In 1996, I was arrested for selling marijuana, conspiracy to sell and possession of marijuana. I was sentenced to twenty-seven years in prison. And I pleaded guilty to this present RICO conspiracy.

Q: You mentioned marijuana trafficking.

A: I got involved originally in the mid-'80s and then I got involved in it again at the end of '91, '92.

Q: What was the least amount of marijuana that you and people you were working with sold?

A: Probably five hundred to a thousand pounds.

Q: What was the most amount of marijuana you sold?

A: Around twelve, thirteen thousand pounds in a year.

Q: Did the indictment against you and the charges against you charge you with being a major marijuana trafficker?

A: Yes.

Q: Were you a major marijuana trafficker?

A: Yes.

Q: You said you are currently incarcerated?

A: Yes.

Q: How long have you been incarcerated?

A: Nine years.

Q: You mentioned a little bit to the jury before some other previous periods of incarceration you had.

A: I was incarcerated in, I believe, 1972 to '73 or beginning of '74, Lewisburg Penitentiary. I was incarcerated in '81 to '83, in Allenwood Camp, and I was incarcerated in 1997, and I started in Lewisburg, and then I went to Allenwood FCI. Then I went to Butner for my cancer operation, and I went back to Allenwood, and then I went to Gilmer, West Virginia.

Q: Mr Kaplan, do you know how many criminal convictions you have total?

A: Five.

Q: How many times have you gone to trial?

A: Twice.

Q: So you have pled guilty three times?

A: I pled guilty, including this case, three times.

Q: OK. In your trial cases, were you guilty of what the government said you did?

A: Yes.

Q: Were you guilty of the things you pled guilty to?

A: Yes.

Q: Why did you go to trial?

A: I felt that I had the right to make the government prove I was guilty.

Q: Did you ever commit a crime in prison?

A: Yes. I was involved in an assault on an inmate who assaulted me and he was assaulting other people, and I paid a Mexican a thousand dollars to have him assaulted.

Q: How did you get the thousand dollars to the Mexican?

A: I asked one of my friends to send it to him.

Q: How badly hurt was this fellow after he was assaulted?

A: He was assaulted pretty bad. That's part of what prison life is all about.

At this time we point out that Kaplan required no help from mobsters in any of his business ventures, legal or not. He made millions selling marijuana, for example, and virtually nothing went to gangsters. He was a big earner for the Lucchese Mafia family in many businesses, though, and everybody was afraid of bothering him. Some associates believed he could have them killed. Mafia danger is the illusion of Mafia danger. Also, the mob families couldn't move in on him because they didn't know how to do what he was doing. He was in crime as a business, not an underworld dodge played on street corners and alleys. Gangsters can't do what he did because it requires effort and thought. Kaplan ran legal garment businesses that made great money and let implied threats do the heavy lifting. Gangsters can manage private sanitation pick-ups or union organising with violence, but Burt's schemes required actual work.

Q: What got you into the garment business?

A: A friend of mine came home from prison, and he needed clothes, and I took him to flea markets and stores. In one place, the people who owned the business were friends, and the guy had some leisure suits, and he asked me what I thought they were worth. And I asked him if he wanted a price for swag, which is stolen, or legitimate. He said swag. And I said twenty dollars. He said to me, How would you like to buy these legitimate for twelve dollars? I said,

I would love to buy a lot of them, and I said, Could I borrow one for a few hours? And he said yes. And I took the fellow that came home from prison, and we drove up to Connecticut, and I showed them to a discount store that I knew up there, and I said, How would you like to buy a lot of them for eighteen dollars or seventeen dollars? And he said, I'd like to buy a lot. I said, The guy has three thousand. He said, I'll buy them all. And I went back to Brooklyn and saw the guy, and I told him the guy wants to buy the three thousand suits, and he said to me, If I bring the three thousand suits into my warehouse and the guy don't take them, there won't be no room for my customers to shop.

So I said, Why don't you call him directly? And I put him on the phone with the guy in Connecticut, and the guy said he would buy them, and they made an arrangement to ship them up on Saturday by truck. We would bring them up to the guy.

And Friday night I got a call at my house about two thirty in the morning from the guy who owns the store, and he said he can't make the delivery tomorrow. I said, You gotta be kidding me, you're going to destroy my friend's business. He says, I can't help it, my roof caved in from the snow.

And I went back, and at five o'clock the next morning we were supposed to meet the guy who owned the business, and we went there, and I told him the bad news, and he got all excited, and I said, You know, maybe I can take a thousand of the suits.

The kid went with me. We went to New Utrecht Avenue and rented an empty fruit store, and we took two-by-fours and crossed them, put some pipe on them and set up some racks for suits.

We took the thousand suits there, and we started calling a lot of people. This was eight, nine in the morning, we started calling a lot of people we know, and we told them we had swag suits and we wanted eighteen, twenty dollars for them, and by one o'clock we sold the thousand suits. And we went back and took another thousand, and by Sunday we had sold the three thousand suits, and I thought this was a very good business, and we decided to go into it.

Q: You used an expression, 'swag'. What does that mean?

A: Swag is stolen merchandise.

Q: OK. So with respect to your clothing business, did you always buy stolen merchandise and resell it, or did you occasionally buy non-stolen merchandise?

A: My clothing business was 100 per cent legitimate clothing. The suits were legitimate.

Q: What do you mean by that?

A: They were bought from the factory. This guy was a legitimate guy who bought closeout goods from factories.

Q: And you just said – you used the expression 'my clothing business was 100 per cent legitimate'. Did you occasionally sell knock-offs?

A: Yes. When you take a label that a designer makes or a large company and you counterfeit it, you copy it. We bought sweatshirts from China, had them made to the exact specifications as Champion and put their labels on it.

Q: And just from 1975 until 1996 when you go to prison, do you pretty much stay in the clothing business?

A: I had some illegal affairs, too. I found a big warehouse in Staten Island, and I moved the business there.

Q: And, Mr Kaplan, generally who were your customers
          for this clothing business?

A: When I got to Staten Island, my customers were
          Macy's, Kmart, Dillard's, Nordstrom and a whole
          bunch of discount chains throughout the United States.

Legal or illegal, Burt Kaplan did not discriminate. One was as good
as the other as long as there was money in the end. There were times
when business ventures started out as legit and then, only when that
failed, turned shady.

Q: Was there a Quaalude case that you went to prison for
          in approximately 1981?

A: I put up some money and rented a warehouse/loft,
          and originally we were going to make hair products
          to ship to Africa, and the chemist that was making
          the hair grease didn't homogenise the product, and
          when it was shipped to Africa, it turned brown and we
          couldn't sell it, and then we decided to try to recoup
          the money. The chemist said that he could make the
          formula for Quaaludes, and we attempted to make
          them.

Marvellous! He should be teaching at Harvard Business School, but
instead these lessons come to us free of charge. And this is all mere
warm-up to the stories he has come to tell. Burt Kaplan saw into the
shadows and understood what they were, for he had lived in them so
many years. Now, after doing so much evil, he is at last committing
what he believes is an atrocious, unforgivable act.

Throughout the trial, Kaplan refers to himself by various street
names for an informer. He is asked what he means when he says
this.

'A stool pigeon is a rat. Just like me.'

Burt Kaplan's voice looses eagles that swoop and scream and
slap against the walls. He carried his loyalty to the Mafia almost

to the end, until he believed there were leopards about to pounce. At the last stroke of midnight, he turned in his claws.

Judd Burstein, one of Kaplan's lawyers, says, 'He is probably the last true believer in the code of the Mafia, the *omertà*.' He is about to become what he despises.

THREE

Even before Burt Kaplan takes the stand, the trial has moments of wonder. They come in a ceremony out of sight and hearing of the public, the questioning of prospective jurors in a forum known as voir dire. This pretentious use of a French title is insulting, for in Brooklyn it is an issue too important for affectation.

Potential jurors are interviewed in a narrow chamber directly behind the courtroom. Sitting at a table are the lawyers and prosecutors, and at the head of the table, in a black double-breasted suit today, is Judge Jack B. Weinstein. An empty chair on his right is for the jurors.

The court officer, a woman in brown named June Lowe, stands in the doorway and with almost no motion brings a prospective juror into the room.

'How are you this morning?' Weinstein asks.

'I'm a little groggy,' the man says. 'I had this on my mind.'

Weinstein says, 'You're not worried about this case, are you?'

'I've never been a juror.'

'Why don't you tell us about yourself?'

'I'm forty-eight and I'm working half my life. I'm a social worker now. I have a son, sixteen. I'm married. Then things fell apart. My nephew was convicted of a crime. There was death involved. I worked and didn't get involved. Then my car was stolen and

I collected the insurance. I go back and forth on legalisation of marijuana.'

'Can you be fair to these defendants?'

'I would like to think I could be fair.'

Weinstein thinks not. He dismisses the man.

Next is a woman who says, 'I actually have three things. I have a son who is fourteen. I have no way to get him to school. You know, I usually drive him every day. Two, I was supposed to start a new job today. I work for the Board of Education. I went from one job to another into another position and that was supposed to start today and I'm here, I'm not getting started.'

Weinstein says, 'I know, but the board is not going to fire you.'

'No. My number-one problem is my son. I'm a single mother, and I drive him. It's not like he goes—'

Weinstein asks, 'Where do you live?'

'I live in Gerritsen Beach.'

'And where is the school?'

'He goes to a Catholic school in . . . I don't know what you call it, the Midwood section.'

Weinstein says, 'There is public transportation. He's fourteen years old.'

She says, 'I know.'

Weinstein says, 'Denied. It's time he grew up.'

Next is a man with an accent, maybe Russian. 'In 1979, I was in criminal court, a victim. A man wanted to kill me because I owed him money. But I got this here,' he says, lifting his shirt to expose a scar.

'You don't think you could be fair?'

'No.'

'Excused.'

Now another woman. 'Your Honour, I wouldn't be able to be fair in this trial.'

'Why?' Weinstein asks.

'Being that my father was always . . . the accusation of my father always being in the mob or because you're Italian and—'

'Was he in the mob?'

'No. But there was always that accusation.'

'By whom?'

'Neighbourhood people, people on the streets of Brooklyn.'

'Denied.'

Prospective juror: 'I have appointments made for the next three months and I don't think I can cancel all of my appointments.'

'You better try, you're not excused.'

Next one up: 'I need kosher, and I can't be sequestered on the Sabbath.'

'We're not going to sequester you. You have to stay here and be selected, and you can bring your own lunch if you like. Denied.'

Now a chubby woman in a black suit. She is from Staten Island.

'How did you travel here today?' Weinstein asked.

'I got a ride.'

'But you can take the ferry or train.'

'Yes I can.'

'Tell us a little bit about yourself.'

'My husband is retired. A knitting mechanic. I'm out, retired, by the end of the year. I have a cousin, a woman, who was in an affair, and there was a murder and a suicide in Florida. A very tragic thing. Florida. My son-in-law is a probation officer for this court. I don't like to know anything about all this.'

There are murmurs from the defence lawyers, who don't want the woman within fifteen miles of the courthouse.

The judge says thank you.

Now there is a man of colour who works as a hospital technician and has three girls and three boys and likes meat loaf and mashed potatoes, a lot of mashed potatoes; then a man from Deer Park who says it takes him an hour to get here. He was in the navy eight years and eleven months, some of it in Iraq, and he is a volunteer firefighter, with an uncle in the West Palm police department in Florida and a friend with a bar in Riverhead who got into a huge fight. Next, a woman with big eyes who takes the Number 3 train for two stations to get to court. 'I have two children, a daughter in pre-med at North Carolina and a son a plumber.' A woman from Crown Heights got here by subway. A child in the army, in Arkansas; a daughter on the stock exchange. A lot of running. Her husband was a butcher. Now deceased. Lives in Staten Island. Got here by car. 'Where did I park the car? Garage across the street. My job only pays ten days for jury duty. I do work.' 'We can see what we can do. We can be very persuasive.' 'I work as a substance-abuse counsellor. My grandmother was mugged years ago. Tough old lady, didn't give up her purse.' 'Are you not well?' 'Not well. Got a cold. Been a bad season. I'm a bus operator. I grew up in the Bronx. I feel I can be objective . . .'

This goes on for days. Somewhere, among the people who spend an hour and a half on the Long Island Rail Road each way and who have two stepchildren and five grandchildren and a husband who likes to talk – 'I've got a talking marriage' – there was a slim woman of colour who spoke in such a small voice that nobody remembers her being in the room. She took the train from Crown Heights and works in patient care at a hospital and is here from Barbados for thirty-two years. She has a daughter twenty-eight and a son who works at Medgar Evers College. She seemed impressive but in her West Indian accent so low that you wondered if anybody could hear her.

They all could. When the jury is seated and sworn in, she is the forewoman.

US District Court Judge Jack Weinstein, who is proud of his age, eighty-four, appears to be the only jurist in the city who can draw spectators. There is nothing flamboyant about him. He brings so much nobility and warmth and common sense into the air that people who drop in on his courtroom wish not to leave. He is also the right judge to sit on Mafia cases. He knows that numbers, as in years in prison, not speeches, are the way to end the Mafia.

He is a large man with a strong voice and broad shoulders, eyebrows sharp enough to scrape the air, framing a hawk's nose. He needs no animation to let you know he runs the place.

Throughout the famous trial of Vincent Gigante, the mob boss mumbled to himself like an imbecile, and his head lolled and slumped as though his brain were severely damaged. Weinstein waited. On sentencing day, he quickly took the bench and said, 'Good morning, Mr Gigante.'

Gigante, startled by the snap of a trap, blurted, 'Good morning, Your Honour.'

He had just blown his act.

On another day, Vic Orena, which is pronounced 'Vicarena', was convicted before Weinstein of mayhem. Orena's campaign for the top job of the Colombo Mafia family was interrupted by Weinstein's sentences of two lifetimes plus one eighty-year term.

'Which one should I do first?' he asked the judge. Weinstein looked at his clerk.

'You name it,' the clerk said.

'Put me down for the eighty years first,' Orena said.

He went to prison in Atlanta, but his lawyers soon entered a motion to throw everything out and bring Vic home. He called Gina, his girl in Long Island, and told her, 'Get my suits and have the tailor take them in. I've lost weight down here. Then go and get me some new shirts. I'm going to win this motion and make bail. We're going to Europe on the first day.'

Orena was brought up by prison bus from Georgia. It took a couple of weeks, and he spent the nights with bugs and rodents in county jails. When he arrived in the courtroom, his motion was a foot-high pile of paper on Weinstein's desk.

His girlfriend Gina was in the room with a suit all ready. The clerk called out 'All rise', and Weinstein entered. The door to the detention pens opened and Vic came in, eyes glistening with hope, in splendid shape.

'What is he doing here?' Weinstein said. 'He belongs in prison.'

'He is here on his motion,' the lawyer said.

'Motion denied,' Weinstein said. 'Marshal, take this man back to prison.'

Orena had been in the courtroom for a time usually clocked in a

Kentucky Derby: 2:03 ⅖. The bus ride back to Atlanta went on for weeks.

Sal Reale of Ozone Park once was a defendant in Weinstein's courtroom over a parole violation. He sat at a table, and the judge, in a grey suit that day, sat across from him. The informality gave Sal enormous hope: He might even let me go home. Then Sal became uneasy. Why are Weinstein's glasses down at the tip of his nose? he asked himself. I don't like that. No, he did not. Weinstein said he was sorry, but the violation of his ten-year parole meant Sal now had to do the ten years. The marshals closed in. The last thing Sal saw was Weinstein pushing his glasses back up.

Judge Weinstein is from the same Bensonhurst as the hoodlums for whom Eppolito and Caracappa worked. He still talks about how people ate in the Depression: food fell off the back of a truck. He was a child actor at eight. He remembers being in a Broadway play, *I Love an Actress,* and on matinée days the stage manager had to pull him in from the sun on the sidewalk. He later folded his 6 ft 4 in. frame into submarines in the Second World War. In the last days of the war, he asked the commander if they really had to sink the Japanese ship they were stalking. 'That's our orders,' the man said, directing the enemy vessel to be torpedoed. Each Memorial Day, Weinstein wears a red poppy.

FOUR

Q: Mr Kaplan, did you ever cooperate with anybody from the FBI until now?

A: I never cooperated with the FBI, never cooperated with anybody.

Q: How many times have government agents or police officers approached you and tried to get you to cooperate with them?

A: Many times. Over ten. When I was arrested this last time, I was taken to DEA headquarters, and when I walked into the room, when they brought me in, they had about fifteen or twenty people in there, and there was high-ranking members of the New York Police Department, inspectors, and FBI agents and DEA people. The police department said, Listen, we are interested in two dirty cops, and if you want to help yourself, then tell us what you know about them right now. I said, I appreciate your conversation, but at this time, without being facetious or nasty, I don't want to talk to anybody about anything.

Without Burt Kaplan, they couldn't convict the cops for illegal parking. His wife and his daughter, who had just given him a new grandson, implored him to bargain with the years left of his life. By late 2004 he was sure that his ex-partners Eppolito and Caracappa were going to be indicted. This could lead to either of two outcomes, Burt reasoned. The cops could join together, turn informant and testify against him in court. Or Burt Kaplan would be murdered in prison.

He could solve all his problems by one sure, direct and utterly distasteful method. Tell. Rat.

Voices were starting to break down his defences. Voices that came back to him from every room they had ever put him. *Tell us.* I'm sorry, I don't do that. *Tell us.* This last time he was in a government office outside the walls of the federal penitentiary at Gilmer, in West Virginia. They had him there because if anybody inside saw him talking to the law, Burt Kaplan would be dead by first light. He had always said no. Now his feelings were changing. He could imagine his friends Eppolito and Caracappa testifying against him on the murders. Unbelievable. Yet he could hear it. Now in this office were these agents down from New York, as they had always been, but this time there was a heavyweight with them. He was Mark Feldman, who was in charge of organised crime in the US Attorney's office in the Eastern District of New York, which was Brooklyn.

'What are we talking about here?' Feldman said.

'I can do my time,' Burt said.

'What are you, the last honourable man?' Feldman said. 'Do you know what's going on? Do you know how many of these guys have turned? I'll tell you: all but you.'

'I can do my time,' Burt Kaplan said. But now his voice was drained of faith. He was arguing with a man who had a letter in his desk saying that Kaplan could get out of jail at once. Suddenly, he could sense what it would be like to be on the outside. He could feel the breeze on Bay Parkway in Brooklyn. Kaplan did not say any of this in the office, however. He didn't have to.

Leaving the room, Feldman said, 'He's turning.'

The Mafia's final hours pass in moments like this, of quiet anguish and betrayal. Once, a gangster might answer such questions in style, as was found in this account, among the papers of Chicago's Mike Rokyo, the late national treasure:

Q: Do you know Al Capone?

A: No.

Q: You don't?

A: No.

Q: I show you this picture. Who is in the picture?

A: Me and Al Capone.

Q: You just said you didn't know him.

A: I met him. That don't mean I know him.

Q: What does Mr Capone do for a living?

A: He told me he sold ties.

Today, step into any federal courtroom and you can't get tough guys to shut up. In the big new courthouse in Manhattan not long ago, you could hear a rat named Joseph Quattrochi, whose confessions are like purse snatching when compared to Kaplan's:

Q: You had a Ponzi scheme.

A: Yes.

Q: You'd agree that you're a dishonest guy.

A: Yes.

Q: You didn't have an honest day in your life.

A: Yes. I made my bed and had to lie in it. It's all right, as long as the bed doesn't roll me into a prison.

In March 2005, in a sealed tenth-floor courtroom in the federal courthouse in downtown Brooklyn, Burton Kaplan walks in with two platoons of prosecutors, FBI agents and marshals. He pleads guilty to all his crimes. Choose a number – eighteen hundred, two thousand, whatever you like. On paper, Kaplan named Eppolito and Caracappa in eight murders that could be proved at the moment, with many more to come, all committed by the men while wearing the badges of the Police Department of the City of New York.

After Kaplan's guilty pleas, Judge Jack B. Weinstein goes over the charges against Eppolito and Caracappa. He tells Mark Feldman, Robert Henoch and the other assistant US Attorneys present that he sees a big problem.

The problem is with the calendar, which has never been stopped, not even by the US government. To understand why this is troubling to Weinstein, let me tell you a little about the federal law known as RICO, which stands for Racketeer Influenced and Corrupt Organizations. RICO was born of the fervent love of punishment possessed by a man named Robert Blakey, a law professor at Notre Dame who wrote it in 1970 for the Senate Subcommittee on Crime and Drugs. He named the law after Edward G. Robinson, who played a racketeer named Rico in the movie *Little Caesar*. Beautiful! Blakey thought that was exciting. He was also an admirer of Senator Joseph McCarthy.

Before RICO, the usual federal sentence for gangsters was five years or so. Most tough guys could do that standing on one hand. And they did. That's why there were no rats back then. You kept your mouth shut, did your time and came home a hero. Once RICO was put in, suddenly there were fifty-year jail terms. If you were committing federal crimes together with other tough guys as part of an ongoing operation, you got RICO. And if you got RICO, you got a sentence that makes Siberian justice look easy.

The language of a RICO indictment usually goes something like this:

'On or about 12 November 2006, the defendants Joseph Orlando and Jerry Degerolamo attended a meeting . . .'

That alone is a crime. And under RICO the sentences are diabolical. For a cup of coffee, you could do decades.

But RICO also comes with a five-year statute of limitations. The indictment must be handed down no more than five years after the last criminal act in the conspiracy was committed. Anything more than that and, as far as RICO is concerned, it's like it never happened.

The cops' last known murder for the mob was in 1992. The indictment was dated March 2005. No good.

If the US Attorney's lawyers tried something cute to slip around that technicality, they would have to get by the mountain named Judge Jack B. Weinstein. Sitting in the Brooklyn federal courthouse, Weinstein for all his life has been a lighthouse in the fog. His books *Weinstein on Evidence* and *Cases and Materials on Evidence* are religious documents in law offices and classrooms. And his thought here on opening day was that the statute of limitations remained in the way of this case.

For an example of how these problems can turn out, all anybody had to do was remember what had taken place in a courtroom just down the hall. Joe Massino, the last big Mafia boss, commander of the Bonanno outfit, was convicted of federal hijacking charges while being acquitted of several more serious matters, such as conspiracy to leave dead bodies scattered around the city. His lawyer jumped up and said that the hijackings occurred more than five years before the indictment. The judge turned it over to the jury. It took them minutes to throw the case out. Soon Massino was back out on the streets, though he would not remain there for long.

Because of Weinstein, I start taking notes with the tiring feeling that it could all be useless. If the judge is warning about the statute's time limitations this early, he could throw the thing out and leave me with nothing.

Herewith to the government's rescue comes the only crooked accountant whose clients might have been more dishonest than he was. Before Weinstein, the US Attorney now states that a man named Stephen Corso can show that the criminal conspiracy kept going even after the cops retired to Las Vegas. Corso himself is quite a solid citizen: he stole clients' tax-return money, then told them that if they didn't wire him more funds immediately, they'd be arrested for fraud. Of course, he had never sent in the clients' taxes to begin with.

Comes now June of 2002, and Corso is driving to work in Manhattan from his home in Greenwich, Connecticut, when on his cell phone a worried person in his office tells him that FBI and revenue agents busted in early and were all over his files. As by now he had taken over five million dollars in tax money, he thought this could get tricky.

So he drove to Kennedy Airport, left the car in long-term parking and fled to his Las Vegas office. And here, too, they came, an agent's hand in every file. Next, an officer walked in holding out handcuffs and asked Corso if he wanted to wear them or – now offering a miniature tape recorder – this wonderful gadget instead. Corso's first choice was not jail. They put him out on the streets of Las Vegas with the recorder.

Swaggering down the same streets was loud Louie Eppolito. Of course they met in the sun – the FBI steered it that way. Corso told Louie that he had two Hollywood producers, young imbeciles, coming into town. They wanted movie scripts about authentic cops and crooks. That huffing noise whistling through the room was Louie blowing the dust off some old movie scripts he had written. They also wanted methamphetamine. Being a decent parent, Louie sent his son Anthony out to buy drugs in a nightclub for nine hundred dollars, a figure that might prompt the law to say it was a crime. Young Eppolito brought the drugs to Corso, whose office now was a control room for federal agents. According to the US Attorney, this was proof of Eppolito's involvement in an organised conspiracy of murder and other crimes that continued to a point in time well within the five-year statute of limitations.

Weinstein disagreed, enough to shake the prosecutors. 'This connection between the end of the action in New York and what's happening now in Nevada is questionable,' the judge said. 'I never heard of a Vegas mob. I've heard of Cincinnati and Cleveland – I'm always confused by both – it's in Ohio. But I never heard of a Vegas mob. There is no national mob. There is no conspiracy between New York and Las Vegas. The evidence is not strong on the statute of limitations. The charges seem to me to be relatively stale, and the statute of limitations problem is going to be a serious one.'

Now the continuing conspiracy required under RICO is hanging by a thread, one that could simply dissolve at any moment.

Jack Weinstein turns to the prosecutors. 'Give me a date when you will have your full discovery materials.'

'Soon,' one of the lawyers says.

'That's not sufficiently precise,' Weinstein says. 'Discovery by July 18th. How long will it take to try the case?'

'Twelve weeks,' the lawyer says.

'Why?'

'We have a hundred witnesses,' the lawyer says.

'I'll tell you how many witnesses you are going to have,' Weinstein says. 'I'm not going to keep jurors here all year. The trial dates are either August 8th, 22nd or September 6th.'

'I'll need three to four months to investigate,' the lawyer says.

'The trial date is September 19th,' Weinstein says.

Suddenly, to confuse matters further, the prosecutor has a new homicide to add to those already in the indictment. Into the long day of talk about murders and mayhem, bloodshed and beatings, snatching and strangling comes another name, that of Israel Greenwald. In trial testimony, he would emerge as the late Jeweller Number Two. It turns out his was actually the first murder committed by these conspirators.

In wonderment, Judge Weinstein says, 'If you amend the indictment at this time, I can't keep the defendants incarcerated.' There is some reeling at the government's table.

Another courtroom appearance again puts the legal system under the lights. The issue this time is bail, which would usually be a perfunctory, rather pointless discussion. The law would sooner put

Son of Sam on the street than these two ex-cops who have been described on television and in newspapers as horrible killers.

But there is a small surprise, another ripple on a calm lake. Weinstein is allowing an unexpectedly generous amount of time for Eppolito's lawyer, Bruce Cutler, and Caracappa's lawyer, Edward Hayes, to argue for bail. Ordinarily, the judge tolerates a few minutes and then sends defendants like Eppolito and Caracappa back to detention cells in time for lunch. Today the speeches go through the afternoon, with no pauses.

The hearing begins with Bruce Cutler about to speak and then purring, 'Excuse me, I'll wait,' aware that the judge is talking to one of his clerks, a woman in a black suit.

Weinstein doesn't even look up at him. 'Go ahead, I'm listening,' he says, just in case you forgot that he's been paying attention to two and three conversations at once for the last forty years.

After that, Cutler speaks softly and so much more effectively than in his loud years of fame while representing and virtually merging with client John Gotti.

The lawyer says that Eppolito had written a non-fiction book that was first titled *The Man in the Middle* before it became *Mafia Cop*. The book, which Eppolito dictated to a writer named Bob Drury, is the smoking gun of crime publishing. It would become primary reading for all cops, lawyers and news reporters in and around the trial. Also psychiatrists interested in suicide. Since you couldn't talk to Louie, you read his book, which for Louie was worse. During the reading, the page numbers seemed to lengthen into prison numbers. Louie Eppolito opens this book by giving up his father, Ralph Eppolito, on a homicide. Louie wrote that Ralph had been raised in the mob by the premier boss in the country, Carlo Gambino himself. He turns in his Uncle Jimmy, too, stating that the Clam had rank in the Mafia. Jimmy the Clam had a son, Jim-Jim, who wanted to be a great gangster but did not know the first commandment: pay or die. He lost twelve thousand dollars gambling and then reneged. The bookmaker was in his seventies and Sicilian, a type whose principles harden with time. He issued a major complaint. Jimmy the Clam paid the debt, but his son's welshing made him look terrible, too. The father and son were called to a meeting to clear the air. Peter Piacenti, who was an ancient ally of Jimmy the Clam's, performed the traditional task of taking your closest friend to his murder. Piacenti escorted Uncle Jimmy and Jim-Jim to the schoolyard of Grady High in Brighton Beach. A deranged mob killer, Roy DeMeo, showed up, too.

So while it was true, Cutler said, that his client's father, uncle and cousin had been mobbed up, Eppolito finished Erasmus Hall High School in 1966 and became a cop at age twenty. At which time, says the lawyer, his client 'turned his back on the family and protected the elderly, the children and was so highly honoured by the police for his heroism and devotion'.

He says that all the government has against him is the word of a crooked informer who moved in on Eppolito after the cop retired. Louie wanted only to write movie scripts and books. The stories on the accountant's tapes were all cops-and-mobsters tall tales in the tone of I'll-break-your-head.

'I heard two hundred hours of those tapes,' Cutler says. He explains the way men speak about violence and states that his client, Eppolito, was merely a creator of canards.

The US Attorney says that three pages of Eppolito's book prove he should not be bailed, because he belonged in a zoo. On one of the three pages, Eppolito stated, 'Bugs never went anyplace without his handy sawed-off – and he fought like hell even when I had him on the ground with my thirty-eight stuck halfway down his throat.'

Back in the precinct, Bugs said, 'Do what you gotta do, pig.'

Eppolito reports himself saying, 'I must have punched Bugs forty times in the head. But he wasn't talking. The guy wore out my arms. My hands were swollen. And he just sneered.

'Finally I took him into a back room and filled a bucket with the hottest hot water I could find. I emptied half a jug of ammonia into the bucket. I couldn't even put my face near it without my eyes burning. Then I grabbed Bugs's head and dunked. He came up screaming. His face was mutating into a giant purple blotch.

But when he caught his breath, he turned to me and told me to "Fuck off."'

Cutler says that Eppolito's talent, 'his forte, his stock in trade', was 'as a creator of apocryphal stories . . . Last year Eppolito told about seven motorcycle Hell's Angels coming to his house when a contractor, a friend of theirs, wouldn't do the work and Eppolito threatened to kill him in front of his wife, parents, kids, friends, and waved a hatchet as he said this.'

The federal prosecutor says that 'words are important, because words are a window into what's in someone's mind'.

Cutler has on a light khaki summer suit that could have used ten pounds less to cover. He mentions all Eppolito's exaggerations while leaning over the lectern and speaking in a pleasant voice, constantly saying 'Your Honour'. Gone was the old Cutler style when he defended John Gotti with a bellow, marching around the courtroom and throwing an indictment into the waste basket. He is now wonderfully understated. For good reason. Nobody does anything except what Jack Weinstein wants him to do.

Weinstein's response to the lawyers' pleadings is to set bail for both cops, five million dollars each, which today can easily be raised on family houses. The New York real-estate market has risen so dramatically that you can put up a couple of common homes in any neighbourhood and bail out your uncle for child molesting.

Later, the cops are upstairs in the courthouse, where two of their lawyers, Bettina Schein and Rae Downes Koshetz, go over bail papers with clerks and jailers. I sit there talking with Cutler when Eppolito comes into the hallway and tells me he remembers a St Patrick's Day afternoon that we spent in a bar on Third Avenue with another detective, Jimmy McCafferty. It never happened. If there is one part of life that I can recall, it is anything that happened in a saloon. While Louie is talking, Caracappa slips out and is soon alone, staring at the harbour water on the ferry going home to Staten Island.

FIVE

There had been so many years when it was so secret that nobody knew it existed. There were the five New York Mafia families, and I heard of some of them only because I lived on 101st Avenue in Queens and up the street, past the old Jerome Theatre, was a place called the Bergin Hunt and Fish Club, with a big plate-glass front window that had a fish in it. Inside were men wearing hats and smoking, playing cards. They were safe, almost completely protected by the ignorance of our times. The head of the FBI, J. Edgar Hoover, declared there was no such thing as the Mafia. The Mafia agreed. Federal agents looked no further.

When I was in grammar school, walking to the Ace movie theatre, we passed the house on the corner where a woman died. There was a tall pole sticking out of a grass plot. Atop the pole was a big spread of flowers. One of us – Elmo Ryan maybe, he knew all things – told us that the house belonged to a big gangster in the Mafia, Vito Genovese, whose wife had passed away. I had no idea what he was talking about.

Then I was twenty and one step off the copyboy's bench when Curly Harris, the press agent for the Teamsters, pulled me out of a bar and off to lunch at Dinty Moore's in the theatre district. I had seen Moore's name many times in the gossip columns. Walking into the place, my feet felt important. Harris had me at a table with Frank Costello. They called him the 'Prime Minister of the

Underworld'. He was with a friend named Joe who was with the Internal Revenue. That's nice, I thought. He has a legitimate friend. Costello assured me, 'This Mafia is a dream so that they could sell it to the public in movies. It don't exist. You're starting off. I don't want you to look silly.'

It wasn't much later that a gangster named Joe Valachi got up and showed the world three-deep Mafia organisational charts.

Because I came from Queens, which nobody in the history of New York newspapers ever wrote about or even saw, I was reputed to be streetwise and tough. Which was untrue. I didn't fight. I chased stories, not beatings. But I knew where to find people who were somewhat less than our civic best, and so editors clung to the illusion. At the old *Herald Tribune,* they asked me one Thursday night if I could cover the sentencing the next day of Tony Provenzano in federal court in Newark. He was the Teamsters' second to Jimmy Hoffa and had been convicted of extortion. They really wanted to get Tony Pro for pushing somebody down an elevator shaft, which he sure did. The reporter who'd been covering the trial had written about Tony's two wives, who in unison called for him to be injured.

So I was walking into the federal courthouse in Newark, and in the hallway was Tony Provenzano with a cigarette holder in his mouth and a group of his guys from the Teamsters. Tony began to mutter, 'Eugene is a friend of mine, he will do it any time . . .' He then punched Eugene on the shoulder. Punched him hard.

As Tony's hand moved, his great diamond pinkie ring glared in the sun coming through the lobby windows. It made you blink. On his way in, Matt Boylan, the chief prosecutor, said to me, 'Take a look at that ring. It's the size of the thing they have in India.'

What did Eugene do after being hit? He gave the same little chant, this time about Nunzi doing anything, and he gave Nunzi a whack on the shoulder.

Now all the Teamsters were hitting each other, and sometimes the punches were good enough to knock a guy off balance.

Tony Pro looked up at me and figured why I was there. He came over and said, 'What paper are you wit'?'

I told him. He said, 'What happened to the guy was here?'

'He took off.'

'They leave you to the fuckin' wolves.'

'They got no wolves here. Just union men.'

It was just a remark, but you could tell by Tony's face that it settled things. He had one eye drooping and the other full of evil.

'You think that was right?' he said.

'What?'

'To put my girlfriend's name in the newspaper so my wife could see it?'

'I wasn't even here. I didn't know any girl. I never did anything.'

'It hurt my wife. I got kids. Do you think they should of done something like that, put a woman's name in the story?'

'I guess.'

'My lawyer says I got a good suitcase against your paper.'

I knew the lawyer, Henry Singer from Brooklyn. He was so sure a Teamsters trial in Newark was an open bazaar that he began his defence by remarking to the judge, 'I can fix your teeth.'

Meanwhile, the one who did make a bazaar of it was Robert Kennedy, then the Attorney General of the United States. He was almost crazy in those days. During the case, he was on the phone asking the judge, Robert Shaw, to read him the charge to the jury. Shaw's clerk had written it. Kennedy listened, then snarled to Shaw, 'Why don't you just apologise to Provenzano?!' Shaw revised the charge to call for everything short of execution. He entered the courtroom with his normal pint bottle of whiskey buried in his robe pocket and an intention to stay out of trouble with this young mad dog Kennedy.

The jury convicted Tony Pro, and now, on sentencing morn, the whole group left the hallway and went into the big courtroom. I couldn't keep my eyes off him. He sat with an arm draped over the back of his bench, and his ring hand dangled so that each twitch of his fingers caught the sunlight crashing through the high windows and made the diamond flash with the strength of a small spotlight. In the row behind Tony Pro, hands gripped the back of the bench, openly bidding for the ring if marshals came and lifted Tony into the detention pens.

The judge, severe-faced on this day, gave a short statement about extortion being an animal crime. He then gave Tony fifteen years, and that is a lot of time. The hands behind Tony itched. But the judge let him and his ring remain out on bail pending appeal.

It was the first thing I saw when I walked into the 20 Green Street bar an hour later. Tony Pro was at the bar with a drink in his hand, and when I came through the door, the light streamed in and found his ring finger.

'I got a suitcase against your paper,' he said.

'So sue,' I said.

I wrote about it all, including the ring. At the newspaper, this was regarded as exceptional. Reporters had written about tough guys before but not about their jewellery. There was sudden new respect for me. I knew exactly how to take it. I announced I was great. Big J.B. Number One. It happened that you needed no extra ability to do such a story. It was all there, like an order in a store being placed on the counter in front of you. A moron can pick it up and go home. Just write down what they do and say. But I declared that it took tremendous courage and talent to do the story.

I had to contend with murderers! Why shouldn't I boast? I wasn't out of some Harvard or Princeton that gets people jobs on their school name. I attended John Adams High School, Ozone Park, Queens, the full five years. Was I nervous about the mobsters? You want to be afraid of something, be afraid of being broke. I remember that John O'Hara wrote me a letter. I made sure everyone was looking when I threw it on the floor. 'I don't need him.' Garson Kanin also wrote. 'Who is he?' I flipped that one away, too. I then went out into the night for a thousand drinks. I went everywhere. I walked into the Copa like a heavyweight contender, and at the bar, Jules Podell, who ran the place, was talking to Jiggs Forlano and Ruby Stein, who were the two biggest shylocks in the country.

'You're in the papers too much,' Jules told them. 'Jiggs and Ruby. Jiggs and Ruby. It sounds like an act. The federals see it and start foaming. They got to get you. Give it up, this Jiggs and Ruby.'

'Ruby and Jiggs,' Ruby said.

Ruby Stein even started calling me at the office to get his name in the paper. I met him often at the Pompeii Room on Park Avenue, where the mob was hanging out then. 'Ruby and Jiggs!' he called out when he saw me. Of course, Jules was right about the publicity. One night Ruby was coming out of a place called the Kiss, and the Gallo mob had a couple of people there to kidnap him. Ruby hooked his arms around the canopy poles and screamed, and they couldn't pull him off, so he lived. Lived to call me up and ask me to write something about it.

Later, when David Berkowitz sent me a letter that became famous, I was asked why this dangerous fruitcake wrote to me.

I said, 'What are you, crazy? Who else would he write to?'

Then it was 1968, in Chicago, when they were trying Paul 'the Waiter' Ricca and a roomful of others on charges of extortion and misuse of lead pipes, knives, guns and stout ropes. I was in town for a speaking date, but I still needed a column, so I went to the federal courthouse. They were picking the jury and broke for lunch as I arrived. Paul the Waiter went for a walk. I went right with him.

'You're from New York,' he said. 'I used to go there to the track.'

'How did you do?'

'I used to go behind this trainer, Fitzsimmons. "Sunny Jim," they call him. When he went to the window, I'm behind him. He was all hunched over. I looked over his shoulders to see what he bets. I did very good,' Ricca said.

I knew for a fact that Sunny Jim Fitzsimmons of Chicot Court, Ozone Park, never went to the pari-mutuel windows, because he never bet. He trained the greatest horses in the world but only once or twice in a year would he say, 'Give me a dollar', and he put up his own dollar and sent somebody to place the wager. His creed was, 'If I knew anything, do you think I'd be out here at five in the morning looking at horses?'

I wrote all this as a column, saying that Paul the Waiter didn't have any truth in him even in casual conversation. It ran in New York, and it also appeared in the *Chicago Sun Times*. Next morning, Paul the Waiter's lawyer rushed up to the judge waving the paper. 'The jurors saw this! They're contaminated!' he cried. As they were talking, in came the *Chicago's American* newspaper, with a column by Jack Mabley, who hated gangsters. He had a piece on Ricca that called him a mad dog. That did it. The judge, Lynch, ordered a recess. He was an old reliable with the Chicago guys. He declared a mistrial in the afternoon. He said it was a sensitive moment, picking jurors, and you couldn't have inflammatory stories going around. All jurors were sent home.

I was gone on an early plane and didn't hear what had happened. 'The judge made such a splash when he went into the tank that even the boys got wet,' Mike Royko told me later. The story of Paul the Waiter's mistrial because of news stories was printed in New York.

Now I am back in my house in Forest Hills one morning when in comes a retired detective who had been good and helpful to me in the past. He said that Junior Persico was going on trial in federal court in Brooklyn, and he had given the detective a couple of mob murders that nobody knew about. 'He's in for heavy time, and he don't want to do that any more,' the retired detective said. 'You could write about the murders when they pick the jurors. Everybody will read it and they can ask for a mistrial.'

Only shortly before this, Persico had a string of federal trials in Brooklyn dealing with various alleged crimes, and each time there was a conviction it was overruled on appeal because each time the same prosecutor put in some outrageous error. Someone who knew about these things told me, 'We got a hook in there.'

I told the old detective that I might write about the new murder cases but only after Junior's trial. When I started to check on the killings, I couldn't verify one bullet hole.

SIX

I keep hearing people talk about the end of the Mafia, but I don't know what that means. I do know that illegal gambling, which once was a glorious fountain of cash for the outfit, now is a government-owned lottery machine that buzzes in every news-stand and deli in the city. Years ago, the state looked upon gambling as a low vice, a depravity, and those who profited from it were no better than cheap pimps and deserved years behind bars. That opinion held right up until the government took it over, at which point it became a civic virtue to lose the rent and all other money you didn't have on rigged games of chance. The states tell the citizens that their lottery and slot-machine money goes to public schools. Never. Tax money to school districts is unchanged. Schools do not get forty dollars more from gambling. The mountain of money suckers pour into the lottery machines goes into the running of government, which means that the mayors and commissioners and councilmen take it.

In its early days, the American Mafia grew big thanks to Prohibition. After which liquor became legal but drugs were desired. They were an exclusive business of the Mafia for a while, but now every country on earth is sending us dope. The only way the mob can again be its exclusive seller is to enlist and go fight in Afghanistan and Iraq.

'Shylock' as a word has become disreputable wherever anti-

Semitism is an enemy. But it is difficult to banish entirely, since Shakespeare coined it with a too-memorable character. On the streets, somebody who can't get the rent or, much more important, money to bet with, takes cash from a shylock. Who will get paid. 'You're getting married?' Tony N. said to a debtor rehearsing for his wedding the next day at Gate of Heaven Roman Catholic Church in Queens. 'You owe a lot of money here. What is this, you going to go down the aisle on crutches?'

Extortionist loans, as the federal indictments call them, have almost disappeared in the rush of people taking brand-new credit cards to automatic tellers that give cash to the touch. When you see people punching numbers into a wall and getting money inside bodegas in the poorest of neighbourhoods, then you are an observer of terrible financial misdeeds. There's your shy.

Once the mob could have a hand in politics. It was possible back then for Mafia bosses and government officials to scheme together. A man with a gun and a politician in his pocket is rather formidable. Today, mobsters are so unsavoury that even elected officials are expected to shun them.

'There are two people coming in,' Betty, the receptionist, was told. This is going back some years. 'A Meade Esposito and Paul Castellano. If they come while I'm out, put them in the back office and then walk away. Don't stand there.'

Betty didn't have the least idea who they were. She was young and just out of college, where she had studied architecture. She had this job in the law office, back in the '70s, until she could start working in her chosen field.

Some minutes later, a short man with square shoulders walked in. 'I'm Meade Esposito,' he said in a raspy voice.

She escorted him back to the office and he shut the door as she left.

Ten minutes later, a tall man with large glasses sauntered in. 'Mr Castellano,' he said.

She took him back to the office and said, 'Mr Esposito is already there.' Castellano went in.

Betty was told, 'Esposito is a politician. Castellano is the Godfather.'

'A killer?' Betty said.

'He gives the orders to get people killed.'

At the meetings of the two, which were often, she never said a word to them and always tried to be busy so she wouldn't have to look.

Castellano, the boss of his crime family, was the man in charge, and Esposito was a loud messenger boy. He was the boss of everything in local politics in Brooklyn and a lot of the city, and he had a rough charm, which was fine in cheap politics, but his true strength was the field-artillery battalion lined up behind Paul Castellano.

On one occasion, Betty was aware of Castellano leaving for the elevator, but Esposito did not come out for some time. She wondered if she should go back and look in the office and see if he had been killed there. She saw the door slightly open. Esposito was on the phone.

'I knew the FBI was around,' Betty was remembering. 'Castellano was friendly with one of them. I know they even came up to the office. They weren't there to arrest him. They liked him. I don't know what that was about. Were they working for him? I don't know. It looked like it.'

Today, the number of Mafia members with long-range money is infinitesimal. You need no complicated thinking to be a gangster. You can be an illiterate in good clothes, and you don't have to work. All through the years, the worst penalty for these men has been honest labour. A neighbourhood tough guy I used to know, his name was Jack, was up for parole at Attica and needed a legitimate job, a can opener, or he would have to remain for the last six months of a long sentence. I went to three people who told me, 'Please, no ex-cons. They don't want to work.' Finally, a guy I knew who had a fuel-oil delivery business took Jack on. That got him out of jail. He came home from Attica. With flourishes, amid vows to the sky of total honesty, Jack started his job on a Monday. On Wednesday, his boss called me. 'Where is he?' he asked. I stuttered, then said, 'He'll straighten out. Let me get at him. It's just one day.' The boss said, 'He wasn't here yesterday either.'

These people are not attracted to work even in illegitimate places. Sal Reale had his airline workers' union office just outside Kennedy, and it was all right, except he had to hire people highly recommended by the Gambino family. Sal had a list of employees' credentials. Typical was:

> Harry D's son-in-law – $200G
> Harry D's wife – $150G

Each morning, the list ruled the office, particularly when work orders started to fill the in-baskets.

'The morning starts with sixty-two people in the office,' Sal recalls. 'By ten o'clock there were twelve people working. We had a lot of paperwork. You had to fill out insurance forms, various federal forms, everything you think of that they could put on paper. We were left with twelve people to do the work. Where did the others go? Here's a woman who gets up, picks up her purse and walks past me without even nodding. I call after her, "Couldn't you give us a hand?" She says, "I was told I didn't have to do any of this work. I have to get my hair done. I'm Paul Vario's cousin."'

The Mafia no longer sends great chords crashing down from the heavens. As it dissolves, you inspect it for what it actually was: grammar-school dropouts who kill each other and purport to live by codes from the hills of Sicily that are actually either unintelligible or ignored.

It lasted longest in film and print, through the false drama of victims being shot gloriously with machine guns but without the usual exit wounds the size of a soup plate.

The great interest in the Mafia was the result of its members being so outrageously disdainful of all rules that just the sight of a mobster caused gleeful whispers. Somebody writing for a living could find it extremely difficult to ignore them.

The Mafia became part of public belief because of movies with stars who were Jewish. This dark fame began with Paul Muni playing Al Capone. After that came Edward G. Robinson, Tony Curtis, Lee Strasberg, Alan King and on and on, part of an entire industry of writers, editors, cameramen, directors, gophers, lighting men, sound men, location men, casting agents – all on the job and the payroll because of the Mafia. Finally, two great actors, Robert De Niro and Al Pacino, put a vowel in there.

It started with great Jewish actors, and now it fades on the words of one of the greatest Mafia witnesses ever, who comes up Jewish. As the obsession with the Mafia slips away, Burt Kaplan gives it a final shove.

The American Mafia was founded when, back in the 1920s, Meyer Lansky, young and vicious, Jewish and from Eastern Europe, went around the streets of downtown New York looking for somebody he had heard about: Charles Luciano, nickname 'Lucky,' equally young, just as vicious, born in Sicily, in a village that was waterless at noon.

The two grew up to be frightening marauders and the foundation of the Mafia.

It then became common for Jewish women and Italian tough guys to marry. When John Gotti put his son in charge of the Gambino family, the guys hollered. Junior was not pure Italian, they charged. 'The mother is a Jew from Russia. He can't be a boss. He can't even be a member.'

'My family comes from Moscow,' the mother, Victoria Gotti, hissed, 'but I'm not Jewish. That comes from Johnny. We went to the track, and he used to give me a hundred dollars to bet a race, and I would put ten dollars in the window and keep the ninety dollars in my purse. I did that every race. One day after a race, I went into my purse for something, and Johnny saw all this money, and he said to everybody at the table, "Look at this Jew!" That's where it started from.'

Joe N. Gallo, the old man of the Gambino bosses, once told a mafioso named Anthony 'Gaspipe' Casso, 'The only way to survive is to get a strong Jew as a partner.' Casso found Burt Kaplan in a saloon, and together they did great until they did not.

SEVEN

Even his friend Burt Kaplan described Anthony Casso as a
homicidal maniac. Still, Burt had Gaspipe at his house for
dinner a couple nights a week.

When they met, Casso was already moving up in the Lucchese
crime family. He was short, a little chunky, with dark hair slicked
back. He began in South Brooklyn by shooting some hawks that
were chasing everybody's pigeons. Then he started beating up
people and hoping to make the Mafia. The only way to get into
the mob was to murder somebody. Then murder again to remain
fearsome, and murder more to get ahead, and murder more and
more until you're the boss and have others murder for you. Casso
had no problem with this system. His one great ability was to
pull a trigger. He was the son of a longshoreman who was called
Gaspipe because he used one to break heads. Young Anthony took
the same nickname and the same weapon. I don't know much
more about the father, but I do know that the son batted right-
handed.

At first, Kaplan needed a friend like Gaspipe because he was in
danger of drowning in shylock debts. It's easy to see how such a
thing could happen.

> **Q:** Sir, you talked earlier about having a gambling
> problem. Can you tell the jury a little bit about that?

A: Yes. I was a compulsive gambler from the time I was 13.

Q: And how did that start?

A: I went to the racetrack with my father a few times, and then I started playing poker in the neighbourhood, and I enjoyed it, and I became sick with it.

Q: You said you became sick with it. What do you mean by that?

A: I couldn't control myself. I was doing every bad thing to get money to gamble. I was thirteen when I started gambling, and then in 1975 I joined Gamblers Anonymous, and I didn't gamble for thirteen years.

Q: And after joining and not gambling for thirteen years, what happened in the late '80s?

A: I went back to gambling. I didn't become anywhere near as degenerate a gambler as I was.

Q: As a result of all this gambling you did, did you lose money?

A: In my lifetime? Probably around three million.

Q: Did you find yourself owing various people money?

A: Yes.

Q: And for how many years in your life did you owe people money with respect to your gambling habit, not like a house loan or something like that?

A: Probably from the time I was in my twenties until 1975.

Q: And did you have to borrow money from people to support your gambling habit?

A: When my credit got used up in the banks, I borrowed from finance companies.

Q: Did there come a time that you started borrowing money from family and friends?

A: Yes.

Q: And did there come a time you started borrowing money from loan sharks?

A: Yes.

Q: Did owing money from gambling lead to you becoming involved with organised-crime figures?

A: Yes.

At this time Kaplan owed money to a dozen shylocks. After a weekend of unlucky gambling, he would awaken on Monday in a sweat, imagining the sound of clicking triggers in the street outside. He had a loving wife who turned for help to her father, a legitimate working New York police officer. He knew a mob leader, a man named Christy 'Tick' Furnari. One day, the father-in-law walked Burt over to the 19th Hole bar, near the Dyker Heights public golf course, and he asked Furnari if they could get all his son-in-law's loans put into one manageable debt. And also let him pay down the principal, which wasn't a shylock's idea of a good arrangement. They wanted men like Burt to pay interest of 2, 3 and 4 per cent every week for the next millennium. At Furnari's request, Casso arranged what was asked, thus saving Burt's life.

Casso and Kaplan were at the bar together from then on. The 19th Hole had a cluster of minor thugs hanging outside and a few major thugs, such as Casso, inside. Kaplan belonged, too. He was coming up as a known drug dealer. That he spent time with Casso was powerful evidence that he could live and work in the lion's mouth.

Back then, Kaplan had a young daughter who dreamed of stepping out of the shadows and into brightness, which she did, becoming a lawyer and now a judge, despite so many nights looking across her fork at a dinner guest named Gaspipe, who arrived reeking of murder.

The man who started Casso's crime outfit, Thomas 'Three-Finger Brown' Lucchese, is long dead but his name remains on the stationery, which is newspaper crime stories. In this the Mafia copies law firms, who keep their dead on the door, in bright gold letters, in order to perpetuate income. Their first lies are their letterheads.

Q: Can you tell the jury, sir, at the time you had that relationship with Mr Eppolito and Mr Caracappa, when it began, where were they employed?

A: New York Police Department.

Q: Was there an intermediary or a go-between?

A: Frank Santora Jr.

Q: How did you meet Mr Santora?

A: I met him in prison. Allenwood Camp. I was there 1981 to 1983. Frankie approached me and said that his cousin was a detective and that if I wanted his cousin to get me information [he] could help me if I ever [had] a problem and could probably help me on ongoing investigations. A detective. He said he – he was – he gave me his name, Louie Eppolito, because I had known his – his uncle. Jimmy Eppolito. Jimmy the Clam. Santora said Mr Louie Eppolito and his partner – I didn't know anybody else's name at that point – but they would do murders.

Q: Turning to the time you were in Allenwood prison. Had you met Frank Santora before that?

A: No.

Q: Can you explain to the jury, if you say you were housed with him, how did that work? What was that arrangement?

A: In prison camp, it's dormitories, and Frankie slept about two or three beds away from me.

Q: How often would you see him in that environment?

A: Four, five times a day. We ate together.

Q: Did you have jobs? Where did Santora work in the jail, do you remember?

A: He worked in the powerhouse.

Q: Where did you work?

A: I worked in the powerhouse.

Q: Santora was an associate of which family?

A: Gambino.

Q: Did you continue your relationship with Mr Santora once you got out of prison?

A: Frankie and I were friends. He used to come to my business and talk, and he also met me at my house and I went to his. I lived on Eighty-fifth Street between Twenty-first Avenue and Bay Parkway. Santora was on Seventy-ninth Street between Twenty-first Avenue and Bay Parkway.

Q: What was it that Mr Santora offered you?

A: He offered to get me information on any investigation that was going on, and if I had a serious problem in the street, he offered to do murders for me.

Q: When Mr Santora initially made that offer to you, did you accept it or reject it?

A: Rejected it. Because, number one, I wasn't doing anything at that time where I needed that help and, number two, I told him I didn't want to do business with any cops.

Q: Why did you not want to do business with cops?

A: I felt it was – it was something that could come back and haunt me, and I didn't want to do it. It would

Q: come back and haunt me with my friends on the street, the friends that I had in organised crime, and possibly could come back and haunt me if one of them would later on in life become an informant.

Q: Did you later accept Santora's offer to pay him as well as his cousin and his cousin's partner money in exchange for law-enforcement information?

A: Yes.

Q: Did Mr Eppolito and Mr Caracappa ever carry out murder contracts for you?

A: Yes.

Q: Mr Kaplan, was it your first murder?

A: Yes.

It happened in 1986 and the victim was Israel Greenwald, a New York jeweller who was also a participant in a crime arranged by Burt Kaplan. His role changed to murder victim when he decided to take all the proceeds of a theft and disappear with them instead of sharing them with his co-conspirators. He thought he could then go home to his family in a nice suburb without suffering as much as a wondering look from anybody. He was somewhat off the mark. He became but the first of eight murders that Burt Kaplan admits to perpetrating along with Gaspipe Casso and the two detectives Eppolito and Caracappa. That there could be more than only eight is at least possible. You get tired of confessing to all these killings and just stop. Anyway, who wants to hear about another in a long line of bad guys shot in the back of the head? These men also arranged and committed a kidnapping. Again, this is the only kidnapping Kaplan mentions. Maybe there were many.

The numbers are unimportant. What we need to understand is only the purpose of these men. Lucchese family boss Gaspipe Casso would tell his associate Burton Kaplan to get confidential information about impending arrests, wiretaps, informants and anything else that seemed useful. Kaplan then went to the two detectives, one of whom, Caracappa, was on an anti-Mafia squad and had easy reach into the police headquarters records room. The other cop, Eppolito, was stationed in a busy precinct where mob guys were concerned. Kaplan paid the men four thousand dollars a month salary and then waited at home while they combed the files and brought him packets of wiretaps and secret police reports. He passed the information to Casso, who often handled the dirty work. There were also times when the cops earned extra money by doing the mob's murders themselves.

Q: And as far as you knew, it was Mr Santora's first murder?

A: I don't know that. I knew that Frankie was a hoodlum. I know that he was capable of doing things like that.

Q: Why didn't you ask the guy, Frank, have you ever killed somebody before? This is an important thing?

A: If I asked that question on the street, Frankie would probably kill me. Why do you want to know what I did? he would say. Are you going to become an informant or something?

Q: Did they ever carry out a kidnapping contract for you?

A: Yes.

Q: What was the name of the person that was kidnapped?

A: Jimmy Hydell.

In the back of the courtroom, a young woman clenches her teeth and hisses. 'Motherfucker . . . My mother wants Jimmy's bones back . . . Put a woman at peace . . .'

The young woman sits next to me and whispers like this through a whole morning's testimony. Her name is Elizabeth Hydell, age forty-two, full of hatred. Her brother Jimmy was shot to death as directed by Kaplan and Casso and carried out by Caracappa and Eppolito.

Jimmy Hydell, twenty-six, was a light-haired hefty thug, an office boy with a gun. He ran around frothing at the mouth and shooting. He was still living with his mother, in Staten Island, when he died. The family originally came from Bensonhurst, on Eighty-third Street, which was dominated by St Bernadette's Catholic Church and school. The Hydells merely had to stroll across the street to Mass. The family bloodlines were German and Irish. The father worked in the transit system.

'My father paid forty thousand for that house. We had to walk away from it,' Elizabeth Hydell mutters. 'It was up for two hundred and twenty thousand, and they came and took the deed away from him.' I ask her why.

'Because my father got told.'

'Who told him?'

'He got told by the top.'

About this she will say no more. It makes no sense to wonder.

'Jimmy was mesmerised by the Mafia,' she tells me. 'The clothes, the cars, the way they just walked around with their jewellery and never had to go to work. He went on killing sprees. At the same time, he was a mama's boy. He called his mother twenty times a day. The night he got engaged, he called her from the hotel room where he was in bed with his fiancée.'

She remembered how Jimmy later became uncontrollable when the young woman, whose name was Annette Dibiase, broke up with him. He kept pacing up and down the hallway at home. 'Then, I don't know what he did, he took her car and tied her up and drove out by the airport like he was rehearsing a kidnap. I guess he was.'

Riding around with him was Robert Bering, a former transit cop who thought that if he piled up enough dead bodies, they would let him in the Mafia, even if he didn't have enough Italian in him to order dinner. Witnesses saw the fiancée being yanked into a car in front of her house. They found her with five bullets in her head, buried near a road in Staten Island. Hydell seemed an insane killer at this point. He had supposedly also murdered two shylocks, one drug seller and two people who ran school-bus companies.

Elizabeth said, 'I was in work when my girlfriend called and told me that they'd found Annette. I knew right away that Jimmy had done it with Bering. When he came home, we all knew he did it. Nobody said nothing to him, and he didn't talk to us. It was obvious that something terrible had happened. Then the next thing, he was ducking and scared of this Casso.'

Hydell and Casso had some history even before they were joined by bullets.

A: I was supposed to meet an attorney, Jerry Shargel, at the 19th Hole where Chris Furnari was, and we were standing outside the bar, and the owner of the Chinese restaurant two doors away came in to talk to Chris, and he told Chris that there's some drunken kids in his place and they had a Doberman dog and they were causing all kind of havoc and the customers were afraid and they were leaving. And Chris went to Angelo Defendis – they all came outside at that time – and I heard Chris say to Angelo Defendis, Didn't I tell you to straighten this kid out to stop causing problems in the neighbourhood? And Angelo Defendis said, I told him. I warned him. So Chris said, Go in there now and get him out of there. And Angelo went into the Chinese restaurant, and he came out with Jimmy Hydell and another kid and – with a big dog – and Angelo started pointing his finger at Jimmy Hydell, and every time he pointed his finger, the dog started to snap at him.

And Gaspipe came along, Casso, and he saw it, and he told Jimmy Hydell, Hold on to that dog and don't let that dog look to intimidate Angelo. And Angelo started yelling at him again; the dog came at him. And

> Gaspipe said, I told you, watch that dog, and Jimmy
> paid him no mind. Gaspipe went into the luncheonette,
> he got a pistol, put a silencer on it, and shot the dog
> twice. Casso told Hydell, Now pick up the dog and
> put him in the trunk of the car and get out of here.

Q. Casso told Jimmy that?

A. Yes.

Like most of what has gone bad in the Mafia, this story also involves John Gotti. I speak of a time in the early '80s when he was still an up-and-comer in the Gambino crime family. His boss was Paul Castellano, who had famously stated that members of his family were forbidden to deal in drugs. The government had bugged Gene Gotti, John's brother, and caught him in a heroin deal. Castellano heard the tape and decided he had to execute Gene Gotti for the big crime of selling heroin and the almost-as-big crime of not turning over any of the money. To save his brother's life, and also to make a little room at the top, John Gotti got the idea to move Castellano into a new home. A funeral parlour.

On 16 December 1985, Castellano visited the LaRossa law office to give Christmas greetings. Afterwards, he left for a meeting at Sparks Restaurant on East Forty-sixth Street in Manhattan. It was only a few yards from Third Avenue, from whose buildings came the start of the rush hour. Johnny 'Crash' Casciola, an operating engineer working a construction job some yards from the restaurant, had just shut down his crane for the day. He was singing 'Fine and Dandy'. He had a date that night to play his accordion for a fee at an affair in Jersey. He noticed several men in fur hats and raincoats in the river of people. As Castellano's car pulled in front of the restaurant, the fur hats rushed up and started shooting. Soon Castellano was dead. The driver, too. The fur hats dissolved back into the throng. Johnny Crash also disappeared. He needed no time to think. He moved by instinct.

A car passed by. John Gotti looked out the passenger window at the carnage. The driver was Sammy Gravano.

Two days later, when asked to remember this, Johnny Crash said, 'What are you talking about, somebody got shot? I was home.'

Shooting a boss supposedly required Mafia commission sanction. There was no real commission left, but there was Vincent 'the Chin' Gigante. He thought, If you kill Castellano, then I, Vincent Gigante, also can be killed. Something had to be done about Gotti, Gigante decided, so he hired Gaspipe Casso to put a bomb in a car parked on a Sunday morning in front of the Veterans and Friends social club on Eighty-sixth Street in Bensonhurst. Never mind that a bomb was also against the Mafia rules that the Chin claimed to uphold. Gotti was inside the club. He left one of his men, Frank DeCicco, in the car. Gotti was supposed to come right out. He tarried. The bomb did not. Mr DeCicco became dust.

As the Mafia always was slightly relaxed about keeping secrets, a hundred people knew by mid-afternoon who had set the bomb. One of whom was Gotti. He had to make Casso go away right now. Gotti told Bobby Boriello, Mickey Boy Paradiso and Eddie Lino to take care of it, and they sent Jimmy Hydell and Robert Bering. To do the work involved in pulling a trigger, they hired a third person, a twenty-six-year-old drug peddler and killer named Nicky Guido. He was heartless and fairly stupid. They hunted Casso in a blue Plymouth Fury that had a siren and a red light on the dashboard to resemble an unmarked police car.

On 14 September 1986, Casso was driving a Lincoln Town Car leased to Progressive Distributors of Staten Island, which was Burton Kaplan's clothing business. Kaplan had given Casso the car as a token of his high esteem. Casso parked it illegally at a bus stop. Why shouldn't he? He was Brooklyn royalty, a boss of the Mafia. He was allowed to do anything he wanted. He stopped in a no-parking space because he felt like ice cream from a Carvel stand. He was also there to meet a guy selling stolen corporate cheques.

Instead, Hydell, Bering and Guido pulled up. While appearing to park legitimately, they scraped the driver's side of the car being driven by Gaspipe, whose gangster instinct sent him crawling across the seat and scrambling like a crab out the passenger door.

Guido had a near-perfect shot at Casso. He had a nine-millimetre semi-automatic weapon and could have hit the man twenty times. But the gun was clogged. Why not? These people live busy lives and don't have time to be cleaning guns.

Hydell, sitting in the backseat, then broke out his shotgun, which he fired five times.

Casso remembered for police, 'I just finished parking the car. I just shut the engine off. When I seen the car pulling up very close like, too close to my car, and then I turned around, and then I seen the flash of the gunfire.'

Casso was hit in the shoulder and neck. He fled the car and ran into the Golden Ox restaurant. He was on the restaurant's kitchen floor with his back against a freezer, bleeding.

The car carrying Bering, Hydell and Guido rushed away, but an off-duty police officer caught the licence plate.

Other lawyers and prosecutors from around the courthouse have come to hear Burt Kaplan tell the story. The jury is breathless.

Q: After the shooting of Casso, did you have a conversation with Vic Amuso about it?

A: Yes.

Q: And, again, who was Vic Amuso at that time?

A: He was a capo in the Lucchese crime family.

Q: OK. What did Amuso say to you about the shooting or after the shooting?

A: He came to my house. I had relatives from Ohio over my house, we were all sitting on the porch, and he called me down. And I went to speak to him, and he said, We've got a problem. He said, They tried to kill our friend. I said, Who? What? He said, They tried to kill Gas. I said, What happened? He said, They started to shoot him in the car, and he's in the hospital, and I want you to go to the hospital and find out what's going on.

I said, Vic, I'm on parole. If I go to the hospital and talk to him, I'm going to get violated. And he said, You're right. I didn't think about it. He says, I'll handle it, and he left.

Q: OK. Do you know what police precinct Casso was shot in?

A: Six-Three.

Q: And do you know whether Mr Eppolito had worked in that precinct at all?

A: Yes, at that time he worked in the Six-Three.

In the investigation file, Detective Caracappa found the licence-plate number of the car containing the thugs who tried killing Casso. He used that to put together a packet of information on the shooters. Shortly after, Burt Kaplan received a visit from his old prison buddy Frank Santora, who brought a present.

A: He comes and meets me with a manila envelope with a bunch of papers from a crime-scene investigation and some – a couple of pictures – and I opened it and I looked in it, and there was a picture of Jimmy Hydell. Then I read the crime-scene reports, and it named who the participants were, what kind of car they were driving, what licence-plate number, where they lived. It was very, very helpful, very efficient, and I said to Frankie, This is terrific, Frankie, what do we owe you? And he said, This is a gift from my cousin and his partner. This is just to show you the kind of things that they would do. They wouldn't take no money, because this was someone looking to hurt you, and they wouldn't take money under those circumstances. We're not that kind of people.

Q: So after you got this packet of information, Mr Kaplan, what did you do with it?

A: I made an arrangement to meet Casso.

Q: When you wanted to meet with Casso, how would you typically contact him?

A: I would – now that I was on parole – I would send Tommy Galpine, kid who worked for me, to his house to make an appointment. I made an arrangement to meet Gas at a social club on Thirteenth Avenue. It was a club operated by a gentleman by the name of Swaggy – he was a made member, I believe, of the Genovese crime family – and I walked into the club, and he was there with Victor Amuso, and I said, Gas, do you know who shot you? And he got very indignant. He says, No, and you don't either. I said, Well, it was Jimmy Hydell. He says, You're crazy, it couldn't have been Jimmy Hydell. I just got him a job with the unions, and we made friends, and we have been close for the last year. I said, Here, and I handed him the envelope. I said, See for yourself.

Q: Did the envelope you handed him have the photograph of Jimmy Hydell in it?

A: Yes. I left him with the package, because I was on parole, and I left, and it was a couple of days later when I seen him again.

Q: What did Casso ask you?

A: What do I owe them for this? I told him the story that they wouldn't take no money because someone tried to hurt him, and he shook his head, he said, Boy, that's really nice of them. They must be pretty good guys.

EIGHT

I have good reason to remember the period in Brooklyn in the 1960s when the family named for Joe Profaci, the old-time Mafia boss, was getting shot up from within by an insurgency group, the Gallo brothers. There were three of them – Larry, Joe and Albert. They came out of 51 President Street, only yards up from the Brooklyn waterfront.

As the newspapers called her, 'Big Mama', the grandmother of the Gallos, also lived there. She would spit at a forest fire. When her grandsons decided to campaign against the incumbent, Joseph Profaci, she sat at the kitchen table and counselled them. Grandson Joey would call newspapers and complain if they did not run his nickname, 'Crazy Joe'. He kept a young lion in the basement. Joey would bring people who owed loan-shark payments to the door to hear the animal roar. The night waiters at the Luna Restaurant on Mulberry Street knew every hair on the lion's mane. This was because Joey walked in one night with the wild beast panting at the end of a chain. A man sat alone at a table while his woman companion was in the ladies' room. Joey and the lion strolled over, and the animal's blood-red eyes glared at the guy, who scrambled and fled the premises. Joey Gallo and the lion were gone from the restaurant by the time the woman returned to her seat. When she asked about her companion, the waiter said, 'I guess he just ran out on the bill.' The woman swore, paid and went home alone.

Joe Gallo did several hard years at Attica. Big Mama remained at the kitchen table. One look at her told you that you were in the presence of greatness. She had grey hair pulled back. Her eyes were sombre, then twinkling and always in command. With grandson Joey in prison, there was little money in the house. With a sigh, she told of one of the crowd who lost his way coming home from a much-needed bank robbery. He was returning to President Street with the money in the backseat of the car in canvas bank bags. The guy saw a hot-dog cart on the kerb on the other side of the street, and he pulled over illegally and was eating a hot dog and sauerkraut when a cop came up and admonished him and began writing a ticket. The officer's gaze fell on the bank bags in the back.

'What are these?' he said.

The guy half choked. 'They let me have them.'

'Yeah, well, just don't move,' the cop said, his gun now out.

In her kitchen, recounting this, Big Mama said, 'I told him, You got to do two things. First, you got to rob the bank. Then you got to get away. He forgot.'

She sighed again. She then mentioned that the police had been around earlier looking for her grandson Larry.

'Why do you want him?' she asked the detectives.

'We just want to talk to him. Somebody was shot.'

'Who was shot?'

'Anthony Abbatemarco was shot.'

Big Mama nodded. 'This-a Abby. Is he dead?'

'No. Hurt.'

'Oh.'

The cops left. Later, when Larry came home, Big Mama said to him, 'Larry, what's the matter? You no can shoot straight?'

Some nights later, I am at the bar of Gallagher's on Fifty-second Street in Manhattan with Dick Dougherty, who was the deputy police commissioner at the time, and Abe Rosenthal of the *Times* newspaper, and I said, 'I don't have to worry any more about day labour with these columns. I have the way out. I'm going to write a book called *The Gang That Couldn't Shoot Straight*.'

Both of them thought it was a great title. Now all I had to do was make up a book. I go home to Forest Hills and begin typing. Soon, I look out the window, and I see gangster Mike Marino's big brick fortress on the next block. It had a driveway on the side onto which the kitchen door opened. Frequently, I would see his wife come outside in a fur coat covering her nightgown to start the car. Marino was inside his brick house, his arms folded over his head, holding his breath. When the car did not explode from dynamite in the starter, Marino came out and the wife slipped out of the car. He kissed her, she went back to the kitchen, and Marino got in the car and drove off to his day's business, which was stealing.

Late at night, I am watching Bobby De Niro in some mobster comedy on TV, and I feel sorry for him because these Mafia parts, at which he is so superb and which he could do for the next thirty years, will soon no longer exist. Al Pacino too. Which is marvellous, because both are American treasures and should be remembered for great roles, not for playing cheap, unworthy punks. I much prefer De Niro or Pacino to Olivier in anything.

Now, watching this movie, I remember a hot summer afternoon when the producer of a movie they were making of *The Gang That Couldn't Shoot Straight* asked me to meet this young actor, Bobby De Niro, because he was replacing Al Pacino in a big role. Pacino was leaving our film to be in another movie, called *The Godfather*. De Niro was taking over his first big movie part.

We talked briefly in a bar, the old Johnny Joyce's on Second Avenue. De Niro looked like he was homeless. It was on a Friday. On Sunday morning, I saw him again. He was going to Italy to learn the speech nuances of people in towns mentioned in the script. He was going there on his own. He was earning seven hundred and fifty dollars a week for the movie. When he left, I remember thinking, Do not stand between this guy and whatever he wants.

What he wanted first was to play gangsters well. Second, he wanted the world. I think he got both. He came along at the end, give or take a show, of the Mafia. 'We had one wiseguy role in the first season,' Bill Clark, the old homicide detective who became executive producer of *NYPD Blue*, was saying the other day. 'That was all because they just couldn't make it as characters for us. Their day was gone.'

Today, aside from needy showmen, the only ones rooting for the mob to survive are FBI agents assigned to the squads that chase gangsters across the streets of the city. Each family has a squad assigned to it. They have numbers – such as C-16, for the Colombo squad – and each agent is assigned to watch three soldiers and one captain in the family. Their work is surveillance and interviews. They will watch a numbers runner for a month, then interview a cab-driver or a mobster's sister. It doesn't matter. Just do the interview. A full-time occupation is obtaining court orders for wiretaps. 'We get promoted by the number of wiretaps we get signed,' an agent admitted.

FBI agents in New York fill out FD-302 forms that pile up in an office. They must do this in order to maintain their way of life. They earn seventy thousand dollars or so a year, live in white suburbs, perform no heavy lifting. After a day at work, they go to a health club, then perhaps stop for a drink with other agents and talk about the jobs they want when they retire. If, after so much interviewing, spying and paying of stool pigeons, they still do not come up with some Mafia dimwit whose arrest makes the news, they face true work for their country: anti-terrorism detail in a wet alley in Amman, Jordan, or a tent on a snowy mountain in Afghanistan.

'What do you want?' Red Hot said. He is on First Avenue in Manhattan, in front of the DeRobertis pastry shop.

'We just want to talk to you,' one of the two FBI agents said.

'You'll have to wait here until I get a lawyer,' Red Hot said.

'We just wanted you to take a ride with us down to the office.'

'The answer is no,' Red Hot said.

'We just want to get fresh fingerprints. We haven't taken yours in a while.'

'That's because I was in jail. And nothing happened to the prints you have. What are you trying to say, they faded? They wore out?'

His friend Frankie Biff advised from the sideline, 'Red Hot, if you go with them, you won't come back. They'll make up a case in the car.'

When the agents left, Red Hot said in a tired voice, 'They'll be back. They're going to make up something and lock me up. Don't even worry about it.'

Some nights later Red Hot was walking into DeRobertis when he dropped dead on the sidewalk.

'He ruined the agents' schedules,' Frankie Biff said. 'They were going to put him away for sure without a case.'

NINE

Q: After you gave Casso the packet of information, what did Casso tell you he did?

A: He had a bunch of people out, other Mafia guys, out looking to catch the people who were mentioned in the report, and specifically Jimmy Hydell.

Q: Did Casso indicate to you what he had intended to do to the people who had shot him?

A: He intended to kill them.

Q: Did Casso mention anything to you about people who might have approved of the attempt on his life?

A: Well, it was important for him to try and get a hold of Jimmy Hydell alive so that Jimmy would tell him who ordered the hit on him. Nobody goes and shoots a made Mafia member without an approval from up above them.

Q: And you said that Casso wanted to question Hydell himself. Did he tell you that?

A: Yes.

Q: At that time, did you know whether anyone besides Casso was looking for Jimmy Hydell?

A: The Gambinos. They had ordered the hit on Casso, and they wanted to kill Jimmy Hydell themselves in order to end it, to silence it, where it came from.

Q: And did there come a time that Casso asked you if you could get your cop friends and get Jimmy Hydell and look to arrest him and turn him over to Casso?

A: Yes.

Q: Did Casso mention any reason why he wanted that to be done by Santora's cousin and Santora's cousin's partner?

A: No way Hydell would ever get in a car with the Gambinos or the Luccheses. He knew either side was looking to kill him. But Eppolito and Caracappa could attempt to arrest Jimmy Hydell, and he would go with them willingly, and then Casso would get him alive.

Q: Did you and Casso discuss a price for kidnapping Jimmy Hydell?

A: He says, What do you think they would take? And I told him the figure I had given them before, and he said, Well, give them more, tell them I'll give them thirty-five thousand. I called Frankie Santora's house, told his wife or his daughter that I was looking to speak to Frankie and I had a beeper number and told him to beep me.

The figure of thirty-five thousand dollars mentioned here was what Casso and Kaplan had paid the cops for the first murder they did, that of Jeweller Number Two, Israel Greenwald. The money is so small for a kidnap-murder that it should be paid in a candy store. The two cops didn't earn enough from their treachery and betrayal and murder to live any better than honest plumbers.

Q: Did you have a meeting with Mr Santora?

A: Yes, I did. I asked him if his cousin – him and his cousin, the detective and his cousin's partner would take the contract to kill Mr Hydell. No, definitely not to kill him. To kidnap him. They wanted him alive by all means. I told Frankie thirty-five thousand.

Q: Mr Kaplan, did there come a time where you provided a car for use by Mr Santora and Mr Santora's cousin and his cousin's partner?

A: Actually, Casso supplied it, gave it to me to give to them.

Q: And can you tell the jury about that?

A: Yes. I told Frank – Frankie requested a car and requested that it looked like a police car, detective's car, and Casso went to Patty Testa, who was a made member of the Luccheses and who was in the car business, and got him to buy a car that looked like a police car.

Q: You said that car that looks like a police car. Can you tell the jury what you mean by that?

A: A car that looks like a detective car, that has the hubcaps with the holes in it and looks like an unmarked police car. I been pulled over many times by an unmarked detective's car. I gave them the car this time and they – they went out looking to get Jimmy Hydell. And they were not having too much success. Casso at the same time had his own crews looking for him in case they didn't get him, and on a Saturday Casso came to my house and he said, It's imperative that we get this guy real quick, because the Gambinos are looking to clip him, kill him, and are you sure your friend and his cousin are out looking for him? I said, I'll reach out for him and light a fire under him, and I did that. I called Frankie. When Frankie called me back, I said, Frankie, it's imperative that we get this kid, because someone else is going to kill him and we want him alive, and he says, We're out looking for him right now. I said, Please, Frankie, it's important. Make sure that you try very hard to get him.

Q: Mr Kaplan, where were they looking for Jimmy?

A: They [had] been looking all over for him, but that particular phone call they said, We just left his house in Staten Island. They had been looking all over for him, and they were going to Brooklyn next.

Q: Can you tell the jury what happened next?

A: I got a phone call from Frankie, and he said, Can you call me back? And I said yes. And I went out, and he beeped me with a number, and I called him back, and he says, We got him. I says, You're kidding? I only spoke to you about [a] half hour ago. He says, No, we got him. Where do you want him? I said, Frankie, I'm going to have to call you back. I beeped Casso, and he called me back, and I told him that they had Jimmy Hydell and where did he want me to bring him. And he said to me, Do you remember the toy store where we used to meet? And I said, Yes, I remember. He says, Can you bring him there? I said, What time? He says, In about an hour. I said, Fine. We'll do that. Then when Frankie called me back, I told him about the Toys 'R' Us store on Flatbush Avenue – he knew where it was – right off the Belt Parkway, and he said yes. I said, Bring him there in an hour. He says, No problem, I'll have him there.

Q: That Toys 'R' Us is on Flatbush Avenue, that is in Brooklyn?

A: Yeah, right near Kings Plaza.

Q: How did he reach you?

A: He beeped me. Once he would beep me, I would go out and call him. I said, Can you call me back? – meaning the beeper. He would never call my house.

Q: Did you ever use any pay phones or other phones that were located near your house?

A: Yes.

Q: Why did you do that?

A: I didn't want – I was on parole. I didn't want to be connected with beeper numbers of organised-crime guys who – or phone numbers of organised-crime guys.

Q: Did you do that even when you were not on parole?

A: I did that as a precaution. I didn't lead a clean life. I also changed cell phones every month or two so that there was no continuing continuity in the numbers.

Q: Did there come a time that day that you went to the Toys 'R' Us?

A: Yes, Anthony Casso was standing about two hundred feet, two hundred and fifty feet from the entrance, the entrance from the street. He was in the parking lot. I pulled up and parked my car next to him and got out. He says, Where is he? And I says, He's coming.

Q: And after you and Casso were there, did there come a time that Santora showed up?

A: Yes. He pulled in, into the lot with the car that we had gotten him, and I walked – he stopped, he saw Casso, and he stopped about fifteen feet from us, and I walked over to him. I said, What's up, Frank? And he says – he was yelling and kicking in the trunk – and he says, I had to pull over, and I punched him to keep him quiet, and you have to be careful that he don't start screaming and yelling. And I took the key to the car, and I walked away from Frankie, and I handed the key to Anthony Casso. Casso looked up, and he said, Who are those two guys at the foot of the parking lot? And I looked up, and I recognised Louie and Steve, and I walked over to Frankie. I said, What are they doing here? He said, They followed me to back me up. And at that time I thought, Wow, what great guys they were. And I told Casso that was Santora's cousin and his partner, and they were backing him up. Casso said, OK. He says, Tell them to get out of here. Tell your friend to get out of here, and you get out of here.

Q: Mr Kaplan, did you ever have a conversation with Mr Caracappa or Mr Eppolito about what had happened that day?

A: We talked about how they got Jimmy, how they captured him, and they said that they went to Staten Island and went to the – to his house and asked his mother where Jimmy was. And I said to them at that point, I said, Aren't youse afraid that she'll pick you out of someplace? And they said, No, we were just doing our job, that's the way we have to look at it. And then they said, We went into Brooklyn, and we found him in a laundromat on Fifteenth Avenue off of Eighty-sixth Street, and Louie said that we walked in, and we arrested him, and he came with us willingly because he knew me and I had some interaction with him before as a police officer.

Q: Did either Mr Eppolito or Mr Caracappa indicate where they brought Jimmy Hydell?

A: They brought him to the same garage – it was a repair or a collision shop, I don't know – and that they brought the car, and they took him out and put him in the trunk.

Q: Did you ever pay anyone any money for that?

A: Forty thousand to Frank Santora.

Q: Did you ever have a conversation with Mr Eppolito or Mr Caracappa about that payment of that money?

A: We discussed the payment and they asked me, Well, what did you pay Frankie for the thing with Jimmy? And I said the original figure was thirty-five thousand and Gaspipe put in a five-thousand-dollar bonus, and then they laughed and they said, That's Frankie. We only got a third of the thirty-five thousand. Frankie put the five thousand dollars in his pocket.

Q: Did there come a time after the kidnapping of Hydell that you had conversations with Casso about Casso's interrogation of Hydell?

A: Yes. He said that they brought Jimmy in front of a bunch of higher-ups and that Jimmy Hydell said, I'll tell them exactly what happened, but I want you to – I know you're going to kill me, Anthony, he says, but I want you to promise me one thing, you'll throw my body in the street so my mother can get the insurance policy.

Q: And meaning what?

A: Hydell had an insurance policy on him. It was not a lot of money, but he wanted his mother to get it. And Casso told him, Don't worry about it, I'll do that. And he didn't do that. He told me he didn't do it. He hid the body.

Q: According to Casso, did Jimmy Hydell tell Casso who was involved in ordering the hit on Casso?

A: Yes. He said that it was Bobby Boriello and Mickey Boy Paradiso and Eddie Lino, and that they got perfect permission from up above.

> **Q:**   Did Hydell give Casso any other information about
>   who was involved in the actual shooting of him?
>
> **A:**   He told him who all the participants were. One name
>   he gave was Nicky Guido.

'One Adam-twelve!' Nicky Guido shouts at the empty street from his twenty-six-inch sparkling blue Schwinn. 'One Adam-twelve, one Adam-twelve,' Nicky Guido calls out in the morning from his bicycle. '415 Seventeenth Street, a white male killed in the street. Murder on Seventeenth Street! One Adam-twelve.'

Nicky gets 'One Adam-twelve' from the television show he likes best of all. He is rushing along on that blue Schwinn, with a push-button siren wailing in the morning air. He makes the first sounds of the day on his block, Seventeenth Street in Park Slope, which is in Brooklyn.

The bike is the first ride of his life, and Nicky Guido is twelve or thirteen. His father oils it, and Nicky washes it each day as if scrubbing his face.

Riding his bike, a twelve year old, riding with his eyes seeing past the end of the block to a sky suggesting that somehow this bright day will turn into the gloom of dusk, Nicky Guido has only these young days of such great beauty that they cannot last.

The music that sings of Nicky Guido delights the heart. The song is of a wonderful young man, dark, slim, energetic and giving. If he sometimes seemed a little slow, if when he became excited he stuttered, he was not slow of heart or of love for his mother. It only became stronger as he grew. He was twenty-six and worked as a phone installer and was on a softball team, and after the games they all walked to Farrell's, the famous saloon that had no bar stools and no refrigerator ice cubes, only cracked ice, pieces taken from a big block in an ice house every day. Everybody on the team went to Farrell's except Nicky Guido, who walked past the saloon door and went around the corner to 512 Seventeenth Street to be with his mother.

'They used to say that Nicky never could do anything big,' Dottie

Laux, who lived next door at 510, was saying. 'I thought being that good to his mother was a pretty big thing.'

Seventeenth Street is sprawling and crowded with people in four- and five-storey attached brownstones. It starts at the harbour, under an expressway and the bulkheads pushing into harbour water. It runs up a cement rise through avenues Fourth and Fifth and Sixth and on up to the block between Eighth and Ninth. Back then it was a block for the poor, the banditos, the drug sellers.

When Seventeenth crossed Ninth Avenue, the street became mostly Irish and Italian. It didn't have much more money than the rougher side of Ninth Avenue, but there was the odd twenty that set the block apart.

On the corner was a shop run by George the Arab, who sold peanuts and olive oil and fresh ground coffee that had the block smelling.

On his street, Guido was known as 'Nicky Daddy', because his father always gave him enough money, a quarter, to buy a double cone from the Mister Softee truck. As he had the money, he didn't have to run home first. He was usually first in line and had the cone in his mouth while all the others were waiting.

It was the street where Nicky had his first victory as a boy. He was given a silver team jacket for the Express softball team. He had waited so long to be a part of the team, been at every game at Prospect Park, sitting on the ground and clapping and shouting, and now he was given a jacket and told he would be a player. He put an arm into that jacket and pulled the rest of it on, and now he was on that blue bike in his silver jacket. He rode the streets as a conqueror, and his blue bike was a great white horse. And at the Express games, they sent him up to bat, and who cares what he did? The only true record they have is of him preening with pride as he came back to Seventeenth Street in a jacket he never took off.

Their summer resort was Coney Island, which people reached by walking two and three blocks to the subway and taking a short ride, ten, twelve minutes, to the beaches, with their vast crowds and the last yards of the Atlantic Ocean hissing over the wet sand. But an adult had to go with a kid to Coney, and on Seventeenth Street men worked and women had the house and maybe too many kids to take to the beach. It was not that simple for the woman to put hand into purse and pay for a day.

So Nicky Guido's cousin Carmine, who lived at 514, turned the street into a summer place. He got a fire-hydrant spray cap from the desk officer at the precinct on Twenty-fifth Street, and at the hydrant in front of 513 Seventeenth Street he used his personal tool, a wire hanger wrapped around a sawed-off broomstick, to twist off the hydrant top and let the spray form a silvery arc for fifty shrieking kids dancing in and out. Among them was Nicky Guido, in the gaze of his mother, who sat on the stoop, and his aunt, who was in a rattan chair next door. Down the block was Carrie, the window sitter, who had the phone numbers of every mother on the block in case she saw something wrong – get your hands off that girl, a fight, abuse – anything she didn't like.

Nicky Guido's Schwinn dazzled the neighbourhood, and kids and even adults were out there snatching it every chance they got, and Nicky's father and uncle, who was a cop, had to comb the neighbourhood to get the bike back. His mother and father would not allow Nicky to ride off the block. When he rode with others and they turned the corner to race around the block, he had to stop and wait for them to return.

The block had one big tree, in front of Fariola's house, and sometimes Nicky hid behind it on his bike, and while the others taunted him he writhed over whether to dart out with the kids and spin around the corner or obey standing orders from his parents.

'He stood every time he started to cross,' Pete Carella remembers.

When he grew up, he took the New York City exam for firefighter, exam number 1162, and also the test for sanitation worker. Nicky Guido passed and was on the eligible list for firefighter, a long wait but worth every day of it, for this was the dream of somebody living in Park Slope. It is a civil-service neighbourhood, with cops and firefighters and sanitation workers and court officers and so many waiting out lists to be appointed to jobs. Nicky Guido was set to be appointed as sanitation worker on 10 April 1985, but he turned it down. He worked his job installing phones and waited for a golden future, the fire department.

Our Nicky Guido was a celebrity on his block, Seventeenth Street in Park Slope, because of his love for his mother and his honesty with everybody else. But somewhere in a night office, a ferret came out of its hole at the base of a wall and started gnawing at Nicky's life.

Later in his dark life, after he was arrested and tried and sentenced to life in prison, Gaspipe Casso went on television, the *60 Minutes* show, from the Florence, Colorado, maximum-security prison. The piece of film ran six years or more after he was interviewed, because the TV people were afraid of using Casso without outside corroboration. Casso said he shot Jimmy Hydell over a dozen times in the arms and legs to get him to name the people who shot Casso that night. Casso said Hydell gave him the name of Nicky Guido. Then, Casso said, he killed Hydell. He said the two cops, Eppolito and Caracappa, were with him. He must have had his reasons for telling all this, although surely he was the only one on earth who had them. He had merely thirty-six murders mixed into his dark hair. He was ready to testify for the government or the defence, whoever wanted him, but nobody did.

You could tell how many people disliked Stephen Caracappa by the amount of time he had to wait at the sixth-floor counter of the criminal-identification section in police headquarters. Someone who used the place as much as he did usually knew enough to call first and ask somebody – one of the women, for they are civilians and get paid very little – if he could bring them anything. A container of coffee, a sandwich, Chinese food from the neighbourhood outside. Offer to bring something, then mention why you were coming down. By the time you arrive at the sixth floor, the printouts are in an envelope at the counter, and you just sign some form and leave.

Caracappa never thought to call anybody first. This was a guy who only a few months before had run a computer check on the name

Monica Singleton, who happened to be a woman he was about to marry. But who says you're supposed to trust so many people, your future wife included?

So when Caracappa arrived this time, he had the name Nicky Guido from Casso. He handed in his square paper form, 'Request for Record Check', and then sat on one of the attached hard seats on either side of the short narrow space.

SEARCH INFO

NAME	CASE
Rodriguez, David	80
Rodriguez, Vincent	80
Medina, Edgar	80
Chavez, Lisandro	80
Sirian, Richard	80
Guido, Nicholas	80

NAME OR TITLE: CARACAPPA STEPHEN Major Case Squad
TAX NUMBER: 562810

All those names were suspects from one of Caracappa's cases, in this matter Number 80. In the list of names for that case, he inserted the one guy he actually wanted, Nicky Guido. Sometimes in these searches Caracappa even requested info on fake names. Now he wanted all there was on Nicholas Guido. He wanted age, addresses, phone number, make of car, licence-plate number, photos, family. Everything you need to track a man and kill him. All for Gaspipe Casso.

Half an hour, an hour, goes by. Caracappa has to wait his turn. He sits under a picture of John Dillinger and his fingerprints. The clerk at the counter hands the form to a detective, who goes to a computer terminal in an adjoining office and taps out the requests.

This is more than twenty years ago, the dim years when doing computer searches was like running fingertips on a cave wall looking for ancient scratches. Inside the sixth-floor office, the detective on the computer is putting Caracappa's request into a system that is both wondrous and ageing fast. Only the job remains the same: find him.

The search turned up two Nicholas Guidos. One was a career criminal, Bad Nicky Guido, who originally came from Bergen Street. That was virtually the same area as our Good Nicky Guido, who was from Seventeenth Street. Bad Nicky's date of birth was 29 January 1957. Good Nicky was born 2 February 1960. Close enough.

The printout they handed to Caracappa showed that Bad Nicky had left Brooklyn, and his new home address was in care of something called the Bureau of Child Welfare, Prevention of Cruelty to Children, Kingston, New York. This was a fake organisation that sounded as though its business was to stop the beating of babies. Its real business was to enable certain people to get handgun licences. These pistols are good for robbing and shooting people, and in particular shooting cops. The child-welfare scam took dues from Bad Nicky Guido and got him a new pistol and a new home address that you couldn't decipher.

Steve Caracappa, who could find anything, was lost. He made a fatal mistake by deciding that the shooter must be the guy still living in Brooklyn. He would find out he had picked the wrong one only when he read of the killing in the newspapers.

Bruce Cutler, defending Lou Eppolito, recalls going over the Guido identification material and becoming mystified. 'We didn't understand how they had something so obviously wrong.'

Q: What did Casso tell you he was doing?

A: He wanted me to – to speak to Frankie and see if he could get a picture and an address of where Nicky Guido lived, and I asked Frankie if could he do that for me, and he said he would speak to his cousin, and Frankie came back and he said his cousin could do it, but he wants four thousand dollars, and I said, I can't authorise that. I'd have to talk to Gas, and I went and told Gaspipe, and Gaspipe said, Gee, I just gave

them a five-thousand-dollar bonus on the thing
with Jimmy Hydell. He says, Tell them that they're
being very greedy and to keep it. I'll get it my own way.
And I was pretty embarrassed to have to go back
and tell Frank Santora that. I was thinking of giving
him the money myself, but I had no way to do this
and give Casso the information. So I told Frankie,
and Frankie says, You know, I agree with you. He says,
They shouldn't have asked for no money for this. And
I never got any more on this from Louie and Steve.

Gaspipe fumed. They had given him nothing he needed on Nicky
Guido. Where is his picture? You got no picture. Where does he
live? Fuck the upstate address he gave, it's a fugazy, a fake. Casso
didn't want to give Caracappa and Eppolito four thousand more
for a new sheet on Guido. He did a thing that was far simpler. He
went to the 19th Hole and found a gas-company worker who was
there to either pay a shylock loan or take one out. He told the guy
he wanted an address for a Nicky Guido who lived in Brooklyn. The
gas-company man went through the billing department and found
Nicholas Guido at Seventeenth Street in Park Slope – Good Nicky.
Bad Nicky was not even on the lists. He was on the lam. Good
Nicky Guido was on the gas-company roll because he'd been paying
the bills for the house where he lived with his mother.

Here is Good Nicky Guido, age sixteen, all grown up and with the
second ride of his life, a Chevy Nova his father got for him.

The young guys of the block who were not using drugs and were
instead marking time until they were old enough to drink hung out
in Joe's Pizzeria. One of them was always working there. Nicky
delivered pizzas with his car. Hustling in and out, doing thirty
deliveries on a Friday night, making a hundred dollars a week. This
put him up there. The stutter was hardly an issue now. Nobody
taunts a bankroll.

Nicky and his friends drove the car around looking out the

windows for girls. One evening in the summer, they drove down to Eleventh Avenue on the West Side of Manhattan, and on the corner by the Lincoln Tunnel entrance a prostitute as tall as a college centre waved to them. Nicky pulled over.

'Do you,' the prostitute said. 'Do you good.'

Nicky was starting to banter with her when his friend Pete Carella, who knew these things, saw the Adam's apple and said to Nicky, 'It's a guy.'

'He was terrorised,' Pete remembers. Nicky got that car moving fast.

> **Q:** At that point in time, when you passed that information to Casso about Nicky Guido and Jimmy Hydell, what did you believe Casso was going to do with that information?
>
> **A:** He was going to kill Nicky Guido and everybody else's name that was in there.

We are at a pause, and on all the computer screens in the federal courtroom in Brooklyn are two photos, one of the older Nicky Guido, the bad one, next to the good Nicky.

Our Nicky Guido has large eyeglasses and a delightful smile.

The other Nicky Guido is older, heavier, no need for glasses.

Lou Eppolito stands at the defence table during the break. There are the two Nicky Guidos on the computer screen in front of him. Just a few feet away, the same two photos are on the large screen set up at one end of the jury box, as if for screening a movie. Two Nicky Guidos stare at Eppolito. He doesn't see them. He looks intently at the courtroom wall, trying to find a sign, an apparition, a voice coming through the wood that says not guilty. He must weigh more than 300 lb. He has the shoulders of a goat. Once he stopped body-building, his front slid down like a slab off a collapsing glacier. He is almost bald, and the sparse hair is grey, matching the grey flesh of cheeks and chin that seem to drip onto his chest. He has the sorrowful eyes of a cow.

Stephen Caracappa is at the end of the table, thin, furtive. It is impossible to decide whether he notices the pictures or anything else. His narrow sharp face reveals less than a frosted window. He holds the left stem of his glasses to his mouth, as if pondering some unseen figure in the air.

The courtroom now turns into four o'clock on Christmas afternoon of 1986 on Seventeenth Street in Park Slope. Bill Laux, of 510 Seventeenth Street, was down the block at a friend's house when his wife, Dottie Laux, called and told him to come home for Christmas dinner. At this hour, they were cooking up and down the block, including at Good Nicky Guido's house. Laux walked up as Nicky Guido and his uncle came out of the house at 512. Nicky had on a white zippered jacket that a girl had given him for Christmas. He and his uncle met their neighbour. Everybody said hello. Nicky took his uncle across the street, where he had his new Nissan sports car parked. They got in, and Nicky was gleefully showing his uncle the inside.

Nobody noticed the large old Cadillac that came slowly down the street. The driver parked in front of Nicky Guido's, and then two men got out and here they came, one on the street side, the other on the sidewalk.

Nicky Guido did exactly what everybody would expect him to do. He threw himself atop his uncle just as the men started shooting.

In her kitchen across the street, Dottie Laux heard shots. She saw heads running by her window. She and her husband came out into the street.

The Cadillac was gone. They hadn't seen it. They saw the heads through the windshield of Nicky's car. One was the uncle's, who was trying to get out from under his dead nephew.

Dottie Laux ran to the car. 'I did not realise,' she said.

Her husband said, 'Go inside.'

In the front seat, Nicky Guido, his new white jacket now red.

He died the hero he wanted to be.

That day Detective George Terra was in his car when he heard the news. He remembers it was still light when he stopped at the Seventy-sixth Precinct. He went up the stairs to the detectives' office and announced, 'That Guido. They shot the wrong guy.'

A: First it was all over the – it was all over the news, and then Frankie, Frankie Santora, reached out for me, and I met him, and I said, You know, your guys killed the wrong Nicky Guido.

Q: And what did Santora say about that?

A: He said Gas should have paid the four thousand dollars and got the right information on Nicky Guido. Gas got it off of somebody who worked in the gas company, and he got the wrong guy.

Q: Did you ever have a conversation with Mr Eppolito about the good Nicky Guido being killed?

A: He told me the same thing that Frankie Santora did.

Q: Which was what?

A: Gas should have paid the money and he would have got the right guy.

Today, you knock on the door of the good Nicky Guido's aunt, and she says, 'What do you want?' She is on a hospital bed in the living room of her house at 514 Seventeenth Street.

'I wanted to ask you about your nephew.'

'What for? They keep bringing it up to torture my sister.'

Her sister, Nicky Guido's mother, refuses to speak to anybody.

The aunt's son, Nicky Guido's cousin, Carmine, comes out of a dim front room where he had been sleeping.

Their neighbour Dottie Laux had told me that Carmine was a limousine driver. 'Late customers?' I say. 'Long hours, limousines.'

'I don't drive a limousine,' the cousin says. He is about forty, short and stocky with sparse hair.

'Oh, I thought you were a driver,' I say.

'I work nights, security for Bear Stearns,' he says. 'What do you want here?'

'To talk about your cousin.'

'Can't they leave us alone?' he says.

'Yeah, leave us alone,' his aunt says over her shoulder.

The cousin says, 'The time Nicky got killed, they had me in the precinct nine hours. They wanted to know if he was in the Mafia. He was Italian, he got shot, he had a brand-new car. Why didn't I tell the truth that he was a mobster? I was probably being asked by the two cops who killed him.'

'What do you want?' the aunt says.

'To talk.'

'Get out of here and leave us alone. Where are you from?'

'From you,' I say.

TEN

Eppolito, **big, brazen and brawling,** and Caracappa, slender, stealthy, silent – each lived with a clear view of hell. People are said to be born with good thriving somewhere within, but these two cops overwhelmed any decency with venom and a frenzied grasping of money for murder, never enough money, always wanting more.

Q: You talked about Santora getting murdered and can you just tell the jury, again, about when that happened?

A: In 1987, probably towards the end of the summer.

Q: Did you have a conversation with Casso at all about Santora's murder?

A: Yes. When I went up to Casso and told him that Frank was killed, he told me, Jeez, I didn't know that was our friend. He said, If I knew that, I could have stopped it.

Q: Was Santora killed alone or with someone else?

A: Was killed with Carmine Varriale.

Q: Did you know whether Carmine Varriale was a target of Casso's?

A: Carmine Varriale was a target. Gaspipe was having problems with him all along. I don't know if that's the reason he got killed, but Frankie definitely wasn't the target. Frankie just had bad luck by being with him.

Q: Did there come a time that you had a meeting with Mr Eppolito?

A: In Mrs Santora's house. I would say, within a month. I went there to Frankie's house, and I sat down in his dining room and with Louie at the table, and Frankie's wife went into another room, and Louie says, I'm pretty sure you know who I am, and I said, Yes, I know who you are. I have seen you on a few occasions. You're Frankie's cousin, and he said yes. And he asked me if I had a desire to continue the business that we were doing together.

Q: What did you take that to mean?

A: To work directly with Louie. Continue getting information.

Q: Does there come a time that you get contact information from Mr Eppolito?

A: Yes. I got his home phone number.

Q: Did you give him any contact information?

A: My beeper number. And my daughter's phone number in my house. Only to be used in an emergency. My daughter was not living at the house at that time.

Q: Did you recognise anybody outside after you left that meeting in Mrs Santora's?

A: Yes. I saw a gentleman sitting in his car like this on the passenger side of the car, almost directly in the driveway. He had his head on his hand like this, and he was watching. I didn't know him by name, but I recognised him as Louie's partner, Steve Caracappa.

Q: After the discussion with Mr Eppolito, did you speak to Casso?

A: About the four thousand, yes. He said, What do you think? I said, Well, so far they've been real good to you. He says, Yes, I agree with that. And let's do it. Tell them if they want to do this and we go forward on it, that they have to work exclusively for us. We don't want them giving information to other guys in other families and possibly have a problem back from it which will eventually come back to us.

Q: Did you discuss methods of contacting one another?

A: When I would call Louie, I would always use the name Marco, and if I beeped, he had given me a beeper number for Steve, and I agreed to use my prefix in my home phone number, 259, and put that behind the beeper so he would know it was me. Louie would come to my house about ten o'clock at night. I would know he was coming. I would put on the porch light, and he would tap on my front window, and I would go and open the door, and him and I would meet in my house. I have met Louie on the Southern State Parkway. I met Louie on the Long Island Expressway. Louie had some form of an acquaintance with a lady who lived on Eighty-fourth Street. I met him there a couple of times, and originally I met Steve with Louie at Perkins Pancake House in Staten Island, and Steve and I both agreed – it was in the parking lot – and we both agreed it wasn't a good spot for us to be seen, because we could be seen together there, and I got in the car, and Steve took me to a cemetery in Staten Island, and then he took me to where his brother lived and where his mother lived, and it was on a block with a church and a school, and he says, When it meets both of our conveniences, I'll meet you here, and you beep your horn, and we'll go to the cemetery and talk there. I also met Steve at his house. In the apartment in New York City.

Q: When Mr Eppolito came to your house, was he with Mr Caracappa or alone, or how did that work?

A: Most of the time, in the beginning especially, Louie came alone. Then Louie and I had a big argument, and Louie said he wanted to meet Gaspipe, and I said, Louie, that don't make no sense. Why do you want to do that? He said, We've been so good with our information, I think we deserve more money. I said, That isn't going to happen. You are not going to meet him. He says, I'm willing to stand on one side of the door. He could be on the other side of the door. We don't have to see each other. I said, Louie, that isn't going to happen, and he got a little indignant with me. We had an argument, and if you look at Mr Eppolito, he is three times my size. And I pushed him out the door to my house, and we had an argument, and I said, Don't ever come back to my house any more.

Q: When did any meetings happen after that?

A: About a month later, Steve Caracappa came to my house with a box of cookies, and he says, Is it OK if we talk? And I says, Sure. I like Steve. I liked him then. I like him now. I am not doing him any good by being a rat, but I always liked him.

Q: What did you and Mr Caracappa talk about?

A: Him and I talked about continuing the service of Gas, instead of Louie. He would meet with me, because he knew Louie and I had the argument. Louie must have went back and told him, and I also told him.

Q: Then you said a certain amount of time went by before you started to meet with Mr Caracappa?

A: A month after that, Steve came to my house. If my wife was sleeping, we would talk in the living room, which was the first room into the house. If my wife was awake, we would go into the back to where my daughter used to live.

Q: Mr Kaplan, did there come a time that you learned where Mr Caracappa was assigned within the police department?

A: Louie had told me that Steve had a big job. He was assigned to the major-case squad, and he was there acting with FBI agents on a daily basis.

You find out right now what a greedy imbecile we have here in Eppolito. He has precisely what it takes to be a thieving, conniving Mafia cop.

A: One time Louie Eppolito was getting a C-note, and he said, I'm going away on vacation. This was – we were new friends at that time, and he told me, I'm taking my family away on vacation, and I'm taking my mother-in-law with me, and my American Express is just about maxed out, and would I – would I be willing to send him some money if he needs it. And I said, Louie, why would we want to do that? If you need the money, I'll give it to you now. He says, No, I really don't want the money unless I need it. But if I need it, will you promise me you'll send it to me? And I said yes.

Eppolito stands on the shores of Gravesend Bay, Brooklyn, about to take a trip to the Caribbean, during which he may need more money than he has. He asks Kaplan if he can provide, and Burt says yes, fine, come and get it. But no, Eppolito does not want the money in Brooklyn. He wants it delivered to him in the Caribbean. And not by Western Union, which might cost ten dollars. No, he says, 'If I need it, have somebody buy a round-trip plane ticket and a hotel room to bring it to me', which could cost more than the loan. The prosecutor asks and Kaplan answers:

> **A:** And he did call me from one of the islands, and he said he needed the money, and I gave the money to Tommy, and he took it down to him. I think it was a couple of thousand dollars. It may have been three. Louie was in one of the islands. Caribbean – I don't know how you pronounce it.

ELEVEN

In 2004, two years before Burt Kaplan took over this courtroom, Joe Massino sits in another one just down the hall and looses the worst of devils, the one who betrays hell. Joe Massino sits in the lights and imagines he lives again on one of the great nights of his life, when he swore in a whole squad of new Bonanno soldiers at the J&S Cake plant on Fifty-eighth Road in Middle Village, Queens.

'You can be proud of being in this family,' Joe Massino told these new members of the Mafia. 'In the history of the Bonanno family, there has not been one informer, not one fucking rat. We are the only family that has never had a rat. Years back there were two members of this family who died in the electric chair because they wouldn't tell anybody nothing. We are the only family that never had an informer. All these others, they bred rats. Not us. Not never. I'm proud of this family. This family got real honour. We believe in *omertà*.'

Joe Massino knows everybody and everything about the waning days of the Mafia. He is a traditional mobster. He eats until he can't fit at the table. He ran a restaurant with the best pork bracciole in the whole city. He flicks a thumb down and somebody dies. He has a wife and daughters and several girlfriends. He lives in Howard Beach, Queens, which had an overcrowding of big gangsters. Joe's house was a few blocks from John Gotti's. And also near

Vic Amuso, who is also wide and, before handcuffs, a boss of the Lucchese family. Joe Massino was known best for picking up the tab and paying in cash for honoured guests in his own restaurant, the CasaBlanca. The reason was far beyond hospitality: he didn't want some agent to prove that he owned the place. But now he sat in court, and the courtroom doesn't allow facades.

Joe Massino is a gangster with a perfectly horrible record of whom something mildly good can be said. As a boss of the Bonanno family, Joe had a domestic policy that gave the right of common sense to the bereaved. For expired mobsters who didn't require secret burials, there was a form of grieving directed by Anthony Elmont. He is named after the Elmont neighbourhood around Belmont Park Race Track. Upon a death, he called captains to advise them of the loss and to command which of them may attend the funeral. He had to balance a traditional show of grieving and respect with the need to remain away from the sweeping lenses that federal and local cameras trained on a mob funeral. There were fifteen captains in the Bonanno family. Each captain had a crew of ten soldiers. A soldier could have any number, twenty-five and more, listed as associates. Any captain who felt it was important for his men to attend a funeral had to clear this with Anthony Elmont. There would be no more hundred-car funeral processions starring in FBI documentaries. There could be as few as one representative per captain at a funeral.

Joe Massino also tightened wedding attendance. He ruled that the bride's family should invite all captains and crews, numbering perhaps a hundred and fifty people in the Bonanno line-up. The invitation meant that wedding gifts were not only very nice but vital to life, with a gift defined as cash. But the captains were allowed to send just one man per crew to the ceremony and reception. This meant that rather than a hundred and fifty men and their wives to feed, there would be at most thirty representatives in attendance. This cut down dramatically what the caterer could charge and therefore increased by sixfold what the newly married couple would make on the day.

But now who could believe anything Massino had to say? All his life Joe has had a religious belief in *omertà*, a stop on his own personal stations of the cross. Joe Massino looks up from the computer that he and all lawyers keep on the table in front of them. At this moment, he concentrates on the monstrous sacrilege being committed in the courtroom in front of him.

Good-Looking Sal Vitale, wrapped in a fine double-breasted dark suit, is on the witness stand testifying for the government against Joe. Sal is the brother of Joe's wife, Josephine. This means he is Joe's brother-in-law. Joe made him the underboss of the Mafia's Bonanno crime family. In deepest gratitude, Sal now talks against Joe on charges of murders and being the head of the crime family. One of the murder charges aimed at Joe Massino could even carry a death penalty.

Did Joe ever kill somebody? What are you talking about? He killed the three capos. Dominick Trinchera, Sonny Red Indelicato and Philly Lucky. 'I can prove it, you know,' Good-Looking Sal said.

The inside of Joe's head turns white with fear. Joe Massino is good and overweight. He is fencing with three hundred. He has a round, bland face and short white hair. The heritage of great mobster suits ended at Joe's plain blue outfit and open-collar white shirt. Glasses are perched on his nose as his pudgy fingers touch the computer keyboard.

'How could Sal do this? Joe taught him how to swim,' Sal Restivo from Joe's restaurant complains. 'How could you turn against somebody taught you to swim? He taught Good-Looking Sal to swim, he don't drown.'

Joe always was a very good swimmer. He could swim from Coney Island all the way across a wide inlet to Breezy Point, on the ocean. Joe taught Sal how to breathe with his face in the water. Then he taught him all the strokes. A lot of good that did. Now he is trying to drown Joe Massino.

'Joe Massino asked me to borrow ten thousand off of Doo Doo Pastore so that when he killed Doo Doo, he wouldn't have to give it back,' Sal testifies. 'I asked Doo Doo for ten, and he only gave me nine. I gave it to Joe Massino. Joe Massino told me he shot Doo Doo twice in the face. Then he told me to clean up.'

Good-Looking Sal was asked what he hoped to get for his testimony. It was a 5K1 letter from prosecutors to the sentencing judge that tells in a fine light the crimes of the defendant and the extent of his cooperation with the government.

'And is that letter important to you?' Sal is asked on the stand.

Very important, he says. Because it allows the sentencing judge to vary from the guidelines. He doesn't have to give me life. If I breach the agreement, by lying, I'll do life.

The murders of the three captains, which were supposedly committed in deep silence and security, were known everywhere right after the last shot, and you could get a play-by-play at any clubhouse in the city. Everybody knew it was done at Joe's command and that he was right in the centre of the shooting. Which was going to leave Joe facing the sourest hours of his life, when he was forced to choose between liberty and informing. He had no reference for such an undertaking. He knew of no way to consider such a thing, because it had not happened before, ever, for he was a boss, and it was unthinkable that he would break the great traditions of the Mafia.

It all started when a man named Sonny Red Indelicato felt that he should be the boss of the Bonanno mob. He could supplant Joe Massino via bullets. Sonny Red was a captain. He went to two other captains, Dominick Trinchera and Philly Lucky, and pointed out the benefits of a family with Sonny Red in charge.

Joe Massino learned of the plot. On 5 May 1981, he called an administrative meeting with the three captains. You cannot carry a weapon at any such sit-down. Joe held this one in an empty building on Thirteenth Avenue in Brooklyn. There were a thousand guns present, all his.

'The minute you walked in,' Vitale testifies, 'there was a coatroom with a little foyer. The minute I walked into the club, in the foyer, with Vito, Emanuel and some old-timer, we were issued weapons, told to have ski masks that we'd wear when we came out to face the three capos. In the closet, the four of us left the door open a smidge to look out. Emanuel had this grease gun. He said he had been in the army and knew how to work it. It fired four times. Joe Massino come to the door, and he says, Don't fucking shoot until you got somebody to shoot. We were in the closet. We all had our weapons loaded. We waited for the doorbell to ring. Once it did, we put on the ski masks. We seen Trinny enter, Phil Lucky, I didn't know Sonny Red and Frankie Lino. George Sciascia said he would put his hand through his hair on the side of his head, it is a go. Massino says, When you enter the room, say, This is a hold-up, everybody against the wall, giving the impression of the ski masks making it a heist. We wanted them to go up against the wall so that we'd be able to kill all three of them. When the doorbell rang, we looked through the crack and George gave us the sign, the hand to the hair, and we, being me, Vito, Emanuel, and the old-timer, come out of the closet.

'Who was the lead guy was Vito. Emanuel was second, the old-timer went third. I went last, Vito entered the room with Emanuel, while me and the old-timer guarded the exit door. I heard Vito say, Don't anybody move, this is a hold-up, and then shots were being fired. I am kneeling at the door. I seen Vito shoot. I don't know who he shot. I see Joseph Massino punch Philly Lucky. I freeze for five seconds on one knee. Sonny Red fell between me and the old-timer. Fell to my left. I seen George reach in the back, pull out a gun and shoot him on the left side of the head. By that time it was all over. Dominick Trinchera was shot many times with the grease gun. He flopped like a fish. Philly Lucky? I think he got shot from everywhere. He wasn't getting up.

'Everybody left. There was blood all over. Me and Joe Massino were the only ones in the room.'

On this day, twenty-three years later, Sal Vitale and Joe Massino are still alone in that room, covered in blood that never dried.

One look at the jury listening to this rat Sal told Joe that not only did they believe all but they couldn't wait to hear more. The jury's statement on the government's case came soon enough. 'Guilty,' the foreperson said many times in a clear voice.

Right away in Washington, Attorney General John Ashcroft directed prosecutors in Brooklyn to start a capital-punishment case against Joe Massino for another murder: George Sciascia from Canada, a star of the shootings of the three capos. George got good and chesty and told Joe Massino that he wanted to have something to say about running the family. George was belted out in the Bronx. Entire flights of stool pigeons immediately went into the grand jury to show that Massino had the murder done with sufficient reflection. That is bad.

Convicted of killing the three captains, Joe Massino spent the night in jail under the Gowanus Expressway in Brooklyn. He thought about the death penalty. They could put him on a table and pump poison into his arm. Death by lethal injection. Joe was told about that. They make it sound easy on the prisoner. Well, the guy fucking drowns inside, and it don't happen fast, and he feels every instant. This made Joe think.

One of his lawyers, Flora Edwards, working with David Breitbart, went late in the afternoon to check on his diabetes medicines. She had gone to the jailhouse, the Metropolitan Detention Center under the highway on the Brooklyn docks. A guard in the lobby went down the list on his computer. He shook his head. 'Not here.'

'I can't find Joe,' Flora Edwards called in to Breitbart on this late afternoon. 'It's five o'clock and they don't have him.'

That was a Tuesday. On Wednesday morning, she went to the ninth-floor special housing unit, called 'Shu', and still nobody knew anything about Joe Massino.

She went back to her office and wrote a letter to the judge, Nicholas Garaufis. 'I can't find my client.'

She then called Greg Andres, the prosecutor.

'I'm not at liberty to talk,' he told her.

Flora put the phone down. She was stunned. 'He flipped,' she said.

On that same 5 May 1981, on a darkened street corner surrounded by middle-income ranch and split-level houses, at the intersection of 164th Avenue and Cross Bay Boulevard in Howard Beach to be exact, Gene Gotti, John Carneglia and Angelo Ruggiero awaited the body of the late Philly Lucky. It was to be dropped off by Joe Massino. He had seen to it that Philly Lucky and the other two captains were well murdered, and now he was responsible for the bodies. On his way home, which was only blocks away, Massino stopped and made his delivery to the three men. They had been assigned to body disposal by John Gotti, who also lived close and was providing this service as a courtesy to his neighbour and colleague. Room for Philly Lucky was found in a place called the Old Mill, also known as the Hole. The three men, swinging shovels, put Philly Lucky into the mud.

The three got a gravedigger's reward: Gene Gotti is in prison for ever. Carneglia was killed. Ruggiero died, too.

Twenty-three years later, here is Joe Massino cooperating. FBI agents secure the mud of the Old Mill as if it were the federal treasury. Heavy-equipment union workers operating bulldozers and reverse hoes dig up the large muddy lot, shaking the earth for parts of dead mobsters. Agents stand guard even on the streets that lead to the empty ground. They wear blue rain jackets with large gold lettering – FBI – on the back. Teams of FBI are performing manual work, digging up the Hole, filling a bulldozer's scoop with loose heads and collarbones. Squads finishing a stint shuck the rain jackets and reveal white office shirts and ties as they head to their cars for the drive home to Jersey or Long Island. Even this close proximity to hard labour is considered a bad day. Only yards away is Jamaica Bay, which runs under a bridge to the deep Atlantic Ocean. Yet the mobster burial crew dug a grave in the Hole for Philly Lucky. They must have dropped him on an old mattress, for now the digging by machines causes the remains of Philly Lucky to come popping up through the mud as if on springs and into the grateful hands of the agents.

The Hole was used for decades as the site of informal burials. It was a lot covered with weeds and mud and tyres and car parts in Ozone Park, Queens. Around it, homemade frame houses were built so low into the ground that only the rooftops could be seen from the highway.

Years ago, the lot would be crowded for Sunday-morning dogfights, with up to three hundred men in suits and hats and smoking De Nobilis, the short black cigars that smelled for blocks. Nearly all spoke Italian. The air was free of the rule of any law except their own and that was the Mafia. The Hole was under the control of Sammy Falco and Sammy Puma, who were good people. Falco had a scar on his face from a fight in the Bright Eyes bar.

Aside from funerals, the lone organised business in the Hole was Mike's Gun Shop. Mike was in a wheelchair and lived over the shop. Nobody knew how he got up and down, but he was usually at work in the back, making silencers that were popular all over New York. Particularly with the people in Midnight Rose's candy store on Saratoga Avenue in Brownsville, a short ride away. The candy store's back room was a hiring hall for Murder Inc. Mike also sold stolen guns and automatic weapons that caused the ranks of rival mobs to be sharply depleted.

Mike's wife sold legal guns and ammunition in the front of the store.

One great champion of the Hole in Ozone Park was an Italian pit bull called U Couraga. He was brought over from Sicily by old Vincenzo from Crescent Street. He was an Italian pit bull, because he understood only commands in Italian. If you told him, 'Sit,' he didn't move. If you said, '*Siediti!*' he sat. The command 'Attack!' required no translating. The dog knew that word in a thousand languages, and he got into such a wild frenzy that it would be cruel not to let him go and chew somebody up.

He had a match on this particular Sunday morning against a dog brought down to the Hole by people from the Bronx who believed that their beast could hold his own in a zoo. They knew nothing of U Couraga. Reputations of fighting dogs rarely got out of their neighbourhoods. Dogfights were not reported in the newspapers, so there never was an account of U Couraga except rumours of greatness, and who in the Bronx could believe anything about this crummy Ozone Park neighbourhood in Queens where they claimed championships that nobody else knew anything about?

All during this Sunday match, people were going to back doors and buying homemade wine costing one dollar fifty a gallon and made with real grapes in a barrel, strong enough to leave you senseless. At fight time at the Hole, the people took huge swallows of the red wine and the dogs snarled insanely and the crowd shouted for dog murder.

The main-event dogs were in cages facing each other in a dirt ring inside a chicken-wire fence. They were left to look at each other and raise hatred to an indescribable pitch.

Everybody in the Hole bet U Couraga to an eight-to-one favourite. This is not a random recitation; the dog always was eight to one. The Bronx people thought they were being given an opportunity to rob a big crowd without even pulling out a gun. 'My dog could fight Germany,' one of the Bronx guys said.

With a shout, the cages were opened, and the two pit bulls were blurs of hate as they went for each other.

U Couraga's teeth got there first. He got hold of the throat of the Bronx champion and that took care of the Bronx champion.

'I won a hundred from the guy with the pieces of his dog in the dirt in front of him,' says Sal Reale. He was out of East New York and then Ozone Park. He can tell of hiding from cops with grand-jury subpoenas for days in the basement of a bakery in East New York. Because his mother knew that he was living on lemon tarts, she brought sandwiches down. She stamped on the metal cellar doors, and, from underneath, her son Sal pushed the door open just enough to take the sandwiches and tell her he loved her, and then he pulled the door shut. The mother remained. Some days she stayed and spoke to a half dozen people going in and out of the bakery. Sal was sure it was going to be trouble, and it was. The next voices he heard were of cops standing right overhead. 'She stood there a long time,' one voice said. 'Sal must be right around here. We'll get a warrant.' Deep in the night, Sal fled the bakery and drove to Colchester, Vermont, where a kid gas-station attendant looked at Sal's alligator-skin boots and said, 'What's your hurry? Are you in the May-fia?'

After the fight in the Hole, the Bronx dog was removed with a shovel and buried back in the same weeds and rocky earth that held those who were deemed candidates to break the most sacred oath, *omertà*.

Law enforcement remained outside the Hole. 'I am in a car at the corner of Miller and Sutter avenues,' Reale states authoritatively. 'That was in the Seventy-fifth Precinct, where I had no legitimate business, because I was carrying a gun. The guy with me also had a gun. It was all right in the Hole, but not here. We had the lights off, but it was the dead of winter, and we kept the motor on to keep the car warm. A patrol car sees the exhaust coming out of a dark car, so they come over. They found the two of us with guns.

I said, 'Officer, we didn't mean to embarrass you.' We were in the Hole and nobody would bother us for this. They asked me, 'Why do you have one?' I said, 'For our self-protection.'

'They took us to the Seventy-fifth Precinct. The lieutenant sent us up to the detectives' room. Right away I knew what this would be. I told the detectives that I was from the Hole. They said, "Two thousand." I said, "Are you fellas sick?" We started going back and forth, and then we settled for a thousand. The one detective got up and went over to the window and threw it open. Then he pretended to go right to work at his desk. We went out the window and onto the fire escape, and we were gone. Don't we get a block when the same patrol car pulls up. I told them, "We never escaped." They threw us back into the precinct. We had to sit with the detectives again. They tried to act like they never seen us before. I wouldn't give in. "A thousand, what are you crazy? Zero is the number." Finally, it took two hundred to get the window open again. This time we run for the Hole, and they don't come in to get us again.'

TWELVE

Had you caught snatches of their shoptalk, you would have thought they were steam-fitters discussing a job. Kaplan, Casso and the two cops called their trade in murder 'work', or 'a piece of work.' It was all done with the smoothness of an assembly line. Their kind of homicide gave organised crime its name. The other kind of crime, disorganised and angry, filled with missteps, left dead innocents all over the city, like the afternoon back in the '30s when Mad Dog Coll tried to kill one of Dutch Schultz's thugs on a street in East Harlem. The site was a day nursery when he arrived with blazing weapons and a funeral parlour when he was done. The shootings in our story resulted in but one innocent death. Outside of that, all the other bodies they piled up belonged to people whose killings were Long Overdue. Which made the Casso–Kaplan–Cops group marvellously proficient at murder.

Q: Can you tell the jury, sir, do you know of someone named John Otto Heidel?

A: He was an associate of the Lucchese family. He was part of a gang called the Bypass Gang. They did expensive burglaries. They did banks. They bypassed the alarms. They did warehouses, that type of stuff.

Q: Did there come a time, sir, that you went to the El Caribe and overheard or observed a conversation between Otto Heidel and another person named Tommy Karate?

A: Yes. Tommy is a made member of the Bonanno crime family.

Q: What was the sum and substance of the conversation between Otto Heidel and Tommy Karate?

A: I had went to the El Caribe that day to the beach club and to see my tenants who had the luncheon concession there, and we were talking, and Tommy Karate was standing with us, and Otto Heidel walked over, and he was playing racquetball in the facilities. And Tommy Karate says to him, You know something, Otto? I think you're a stool pigeon. And Otto Heidel got very affronted by it. He said, Why are you talking like that, Tommy? And Tommy says, It just seems that every time we do something when you're involved, somebody gets pinched or they know we're coming in before we get there and nothing ever goes right. I personally think you're a stool pigeon.

Q: What else was Otto's reaction besides denying it?

A: To me he looked like he was a little afraid. Tommy Karate was the type of guy that was very, very capable of killing him.

Q: Had you been involved in a watch deal or Bulova watch deal?

A: Yes.

Q: Can you tell the jury, was that related somehow to Otto Heidel?

A: What had happened just before that, Casso told me that this same gang had broken into Bulova's warehouse in Queens and that if I wanted, he could get me the watches from that burglary to fence. And it was a fairly reasonable price, and I said OK, I would do it. And he said, Don't worry about the money, I'll vouch for the money, and we were delivered a truckload of Bulova watches, and Otto Heidel was one of the people who delivered it to Tommy in Staten Island. We had a house we used as a drop there, and Tommy said that there was three or four guys on the truck, and when Tommy came back and told me that, I said to Tommy, Let's do ourselves a favour and load that stuff up and take it to a different spot. And the next day, law enforcement went to that first spot and were looking for the Bulova watches, but they weren't there. People that were involved in the Bulova watches were arrested.

Q: After hearing that conversation between Mr Karate and Mr Heidel, did you inform Casso about it?

A: I told him exactly what happened, the exchanges between the two of them, and I said, You know, I know you're close to this Otto Heidel, and he says, Yes, we've been friends and doing things together for years. We never had no problems with him. I said, To me it didn't look right, the conversation. He said, Well, why don't you ask our friends to find out what they could about Otto? They came back and Louie told me that Otto Heidel was hot. It means he was cooperating.

Q: What did Casso say?

A: What he normally says: Are you sure? I know this guy a long time. Do you think these guys are accurate? I don't know, I says, they haven't told us anything that wasn't accurate yet. He said, OK. I'll take care of it.

Q: What did you take that to mean? When Casso said he would take care of it?

A: Someone had given Otto flat tyres. While he was fixing it, he got shot.

Q: Do you know what precinct Otto Heidel was killed in?

A: Sixty-third.

Q: Did Mr Eppolito give you information about that investigation?

A: He came to my house, and he handed me two mini-tapes, and he said, This will prove that I was right, that the guy was cooperating and that he was taping people. And I didn't have a tape player to play that, and I gave the tapes to Casso. Louie said, I got them out of Otto's apartment while I was doing the investigation and I put them in my boot. His boot, his shoe, his boots. He wore boots.

Q: Did Eppolito indicate to you that he knew where Otto Heidel lived?

A: Yes. It was sure he was there. It was a crime scene. He went to it. He told me he got the tapes from his apartment. I gave them to Anthony Casso. He said, You were right. There is a conversation from a bank burglary and Vic Amuso's voice is on the tape, saying to Otto, Do you want anything? It was a cold night. And Otto was in a van listening to police radios, and Otto said, Yes, soup.

Q: Sir, can you tell the jury, who was Peter Savino?

A: Peter Savino was an associate of the Genovese crime family. He and Anthony Casso were partners in a marijuana business and then a windows business.

Q: Did there come a time that you received information about Mr Savino from either Mr Eppolito or Mr Caracappa?

A: Yes. I believe it was from Louis Eppolito. Louie brought me a piece of paper, a report, a police report, and it said that Pete Savino was cooperating with the government, that he was cooperating with them for a few years, and that he was cooperating originally with a detective in the Sixty-second precinct and that when the government came to Savino and started asking the questions about the window business, he took them immediately down to the basement, where he showed them some bodies buried.

Q: Did Mr Eppolito indicate to you what precinct he had gotten that information from and how he had gotten it?

A: No.

Q: You mentioned some paperwork?

A: It was a report of the background of the whole interview with Pete Savino, that he was originally an informant with somebody in the Sixty-second.

Q: What did you do with that information about Mr Savino?

A: I gave it to Anthony Casso.

Q: Did Savino have a nickname that you remember?

A: 'Black Pete.'

Q: Did there come a time that Casso told you what he did with the report?

A: He gave it to Benny Eggs Mangano, who was high up in the Genovese crime family. Benny Eggs came back about a week later and said that they took Black Pete down into a basement, they put a gun into his mouth, and that he believed and that the other people in the Genovese family believed that Pete wasn't an informant.

Q: Did Mr Eppolito ever make a statement to you regarding about whether he liked working with you?

A: He said that he liked doing things with us, because when he gave us information, people got taken care of that deserved it and that in the past he gave information to other people and they never acted on it. When he gave us information about an informant and eventually the guy got killed, that's the context that I take it in.

Q: And you also mentioned somebody named Dominick Costa?

A: Yes. Louie came and told me that there's a guy by the name of Dominick Costa that's involved in the Bypass Gang that's cooperating. I passed the information to Anthony Casso.

Q: What did Casso say?

A: He said he was going to go see Carmine Sessa and another gentleman by the name of Fusco – I don't remember his first name – and tell them, they were his bosses.

Q: Did anything happen to Costa?

A: Someone followed him into his apartment and shot him in the back of the head, but he lived.

Q: Have you heard of James Bishop?

A: Yes. He was active in the painters' union. He was an associate with the Lucchese crime family. They controlled the union. Bishop was their man.

Q: Did Casso express some concern regarding Bishop to you?

A: Yes. He says that Bishop is acting funny, they sent for him a couple of times, he didn't come, he didn't put the right people to work that he was supposed to on certain jobs, and he asked me to find out if there was any cooperation with the government from Bishop. Ask your two friends if they could find out.

Q: What did you do?

A: I spoke to Louie or Steve, I don't remember at this particular occasion, and I got back an answer that he was cooperating. Casso didn't tell me what he was going to do with it, but within a couple of weeks James Bishop was killed.

Q: Do you recognise that photograph?

A: Yes. Anthony Dilapi. He was in Allenwood with me. Casso asked me to try and get my friends if they could locate him, and I said, I think there's a way to locate him. I said, He's on parole, he was still in prison when I came home, and if we write to his parole officer, we can get his address.

Q: Why did you think Dilapi was on parole?

A: Because he came home from jail after me, and I was on parole.

Q: Did you know specifically the terms of his parole?

A: No. But I knew he was on parole. Casso called for Anthony Dilapi to come in and tell him what he controlled up in the Bronx. Anthony Dilapi was a made member in the Lucchese crime family. He was into the Joker Poker machines and bookmaking places, and Anthony Dilapi said he would come in the following week and give Casso that information. Instead, he sold all his stops, and he left town.

Q: And what did Casso ask you to do with respect to Dilapi?

A: Find him. I suggested that we could find him by contacting his parole officer. I asked Steve if he could write a letter to Dilapi's parole officer, because when you leave one jurisdiction and go to another, you have to be assigned to a different parole officer, and he said he could do that. Again, I asked him, Steve, will this come back and hurt you in the future because it's going to be a permanent record? And he says no, he's not worried about it. He could do it.

Q: Was there any talk by Mr Caracappa of putting Mr Dilapi into an investigation?

A: That's how he said he always did it, whether it be phone numbers or addresses, he would always put it into an ongoing current investigation. He would put the name in with five or six other people in a real investigation going on at that time.

Q: Did there come a time that Mr Caracappa actually gave you information regarding Mr Dilapi?

A: Yes, he did. That he had moved to California and he was involved in some kind of business there, and he gave me an address. I passed it on to Anthony Casso. He told me that he sent three guys out there to kill Dilapi and that he thinks Dilapi spotted one of them that he knew and he moved to a different place.

Q: Did Casso ask you to do anything else?

A: Yes. He asked me if I could speak to my friend and ask him if he could get an updated address of him. I said, I think that's dangerous for him to do that, but I'll ask him anyway. And I spoke with Steve, and I said, Steve, please, if this is going to come back and haunt you, don't do it. Like always, Steve said, I could do it, and he did it. He gave me his new address.

Q: Where was the address?

A: In California, a different building.

Q: Did you have a conversation with Casso after you gave Casso the second address for Dilapi that you had gotten from Mr Caracappa?

A: Yes. He told me that Anthony Dilapi was killed.

Q: Do you know someone named Bruno Facciola?

A: He was a capo in the Lucchese crime family. He was a shylock. From Canarsie.

Q: Did you know of any of Facciola's associates?

A: A fellow by the name of Taylor and a fellow by the name of Visconti.

Q: Did you ever have a conversation with Mr Eppolito or Mr Caracappa regarding Mr Bruno Facciola?

A: Louie Eppolito said that a friend of his owes Bruno Facciola some money, and this is the same kid that has the auto-repair business or the auto-collision business, I don't know what it was, that let us use his place and that Bruno Facciola is pressing him and abusing him, and would I speak to Casso to speak to Facciola and get him to take the pressure off the kid because the kid is a good kid. Casso thought about it for a few minutes, and he said he would speak to Bruno. He said that he spoke to Bruno and Bruno gave him a little bit of a hard time but finally he agreed to do what Casso asked.

Q: What did Mr Eppolito respond?

A: Yes, tell him that he appreciates it very much.

Q: Does there come a time later that Mr Eppolito brings Mr Facciola's name up again?

A: Yes. He said there is an arrest coming down, a big investigation in the jewellery district uptown, and that Bruno Facciola is an unindicted co-conspirator in this oncoming arrest and that he believes that Bruno is hot.

Q: What did you do with respect to that information on Mr Facciola?

A: I brought it to Anthony Casso.

Q: What did Casso say?

A: You got to be kidding me. I know Bruno a lot of years. He says, Are you sure that your friend isn't just trying to get even with Bruno based on the fact that he was abusing his friend, the kid with the repair shop? And I said, No, I brought that up to Louie myself, and he says that Bruno is definitely hot. And Casso says, Well, at this point I got to believe him, because they've been believable on everything else.

Q: Does there come a time that something happens to Facciola?

A: He gets killed.

Q: After Mr Facciola was killed, did you get any information from either Mr Eppolito or Mr Caracappa regarding some friends or associates of Mr Facciola?

A: Louie Eppolito says there is word going around the precinct that Visconti and Taylor said that whoever did this to Bruno better be careful. They were associates of Bruno Facciola. I told it to Casso. First Casso said, We don't have to watch out. They'd better watch out. And then within a month they were both dead.

Q: Have you ever heard the name Gus Ferace?

A: He was an associate, he was a drug dealer, in the Bronx section of the Luccheses, with John Petrocelli and Mike Salerno.

Q: Mr Petrocelli and Mr Salerno, are they Lucchese members?

A: Mr Salerno was at the time. Mr Petrocelli was an associate who later became a made member.

Q: Have you ever heard the name Everett Hatcher?

A: He was a DEA agent. Gus Ferace killed him.

Q: Did Casso tell you anything regarding Gus Ferace and Petrocelli?

A: He told me that the agents were coming around to every club and every bar and every family and telling them whoever is harbouring Ferace is going to have a big problem, and whoever has him should throw him in the street, and Casso told me that Petrocelli was harbouring him.

Q: What do you mean by 'throw him in the street'?

A: Just either kill him or put him out for the agents to catch him. What happened was, Casso told Mikey Salerno to tell Petrocelli to throw Gus Ferace out and to cut him loose and not to harbour him.

Q: Did you later get information regarding Petrocelli?

A: I was given a picture of Mikey Salerno with John Petrocelli. It was taken after Mikey Salerno said that he chased John Petrocelli, who didn't get rid of Ferace. Petrocelli liked him. Ferace was his friend, and he didn't want to listen.

Q: Where did you get the picture from?

A: Louis Eppolito.

Q: What did you do with that information?

A: I gave it to Anthony Casso. He told me that Mike Salerno told him that he had chased Petrocelli and he didn't. He would straighten out the problem with Mike Salerno.

Q: Did anything happen to Salerno and/or Petrocelli?

A: Mike Salerno was killed.

Q: Was it after or before you gave the photograph that you had gotten from Mr Eppolito to Mr Casso?

A: It was definitely after the photograph.

Q: Did anything happen to Mr Petrocelli?

A: He was chased.

THIRTEEN

The horse came into the bar after work and had a drink.

I can say that he was a very brave horse, because he had just left half of South Queens destitute. He ran, and not well, in the last race at Aqueduct Racetrack, just up the avenue.

I can't tell you the exact dates, a thousand bookkeepers couldn't keep track of all this. But the place was Pep McGuire's, the greatest bar in the history of the city. I can tell you that Jimmy Burke put an ice bucket of water on the bar, and the sound of the horse slapping his tongue on that water was heard over voices angry at him for busting them out.

Burke was the highly popular commander of the $6 million Lufthansa robbery at Kennedy Airport. He plotted it from his room in a halfway house, the Hotel Breslin, on Broadway in Manhattan. Of course, they stole my name.

Riding the horse was the immensely disliked jockey Con Errico, who was known in American sport as 'Scamp'. Most in the bar wanted to see Scamp Errico die, and some of them had the pedigree to cause this.

On this night, Errico rode the horse into the middle of the dance floor, and the band played, and people clamoured for Errico's head.

When you look back on it, the whole night was nothing but another episode in our insane asylum. Oh, yes, put the word 'our' in there.

This all happened at a time when the air rippled with the last freedom to take everything and earn nothing. The old white neighbourhoods and factories were looking at changes in the law and in the colour of new people now crowding into old neighbourhoods. It was in low-density Queens, where people going to work on the subway said, 'I'm going to the city', thus identifying their place as second class.

Today, we have no saloons filled with mob guys to make people breathless as they look around and see who's drinking next to them. Could it be that we have so many of the guys in prison that there aren't enough left to crowd a bar? When you add up Mafia indictments of 20 and even 30 hoodlums at a time, you suspect that this is the case. It is at least disappointing. You can drink with legitimate people if you want. I come out of the nights where Fat Tony Salerno, the Tip O'Neill of the underworld, looked around in the Copacabana Lounge, where he drank highballs, and scowled at me. 'Didn't you go where I told you to?' he asks. He is bringing up a moment earlier that day in court when he called me over to the defence table and said loudly in front of judge and jury, 'You look like a bum. I'm embarrassed you dress like this. Here.' He gave me the business card from a tailor on the East Side. 'Tell him you want a suit made right away so you don't make me ashamed I know you.' There is none of that any more. Fat Tony happens to be dead, and he took the style with him. Among the saloons of the city today, there are no notorious places known as mob joints. And there are no more meetings between reporters and gangsters in places known for tough guys and neon and loud fun. News reporters get their information from Jerry Capeci's Gang Land on the Internet. When their work is done, you find reporters at health clubs or going home to some suburb where they drink wine and the contest is who causes more boredom, the wife or the husband.

I stand on Queens Boulevard in front of what was once Pep McGuire's and I recall nights and crimes and I am certain that I hold memories possessed by virtually no one else alive.

The owners were Norton Peppis – known as Pep, he gambled anything he had or didn't have – and Johnny McGuire, who appeared to have started life legitimately by going on the police force. He was in the Seventeenth Precinct and was posted at the door to UN ambassador Henry Cabot Lodge's suite at the Waldorf-Astoria. There had been threats. Officer McGuire, all tuckered out from a day at Monmouth Park Racetrack, took a chair in front of the suite's door and passed out. A flash from a *Daily News* camera woke him up. He tore down the hall after the photographer and begged him to take another picture to preserve his job. The guy gave Johnny a break and let him pose at the door. Beautiful, Johnny said.

In the morning, the police commissioner happened to differ. On his desk was the *Daily News* with a front page featuring Officer Johnny McGuire, uniform collar tugged open, hat and gun on the chair next to him.

The partners opened a barren joint and filled the bar with stewardesses from the nearby airports and lugged in jockeys from Aqueduct, and soon the place was bedlam. Somewhere at the bar was Fat Thomas, drinking and yelling. There was a band, a dance floor and people tumbling around. You had Eddie 'Lockjaw' Davis, saxophonist from the Basie band, drinking scotch and milk at the bar.

Into McGuire's one night walked Bob Price, the deputy mayor of the city, with Abe Rosenthal, the editor of the *New York Times*.

They were here to catch me in what they were sure was fraud. There could be no such place as the one I had been writing so wildly about.

They came brazenly, using a city car and chauffeur.

Fat Thomas was behind the bar as they came in. Roaring. He had tired of waiting for drinks and was taking care of himself.

'Yez want a drink, fellas?' he said.

They ordered. Fat Thomas poured two big scotches and then held them up, one after the other, and swallowed both.

Then he took the two men back into the office, where his friend, a man named Cousin, sat cleaning an automatic weapon used for robbing banks.

'What's up?' Cousin said.

'They wanted to meet you,' Fat Thomas said.

The two remained silent. They went back to the bar and started swallowing what ever was put in front of them.

Rosenthal was dazzled. 'It's all true,' he said. 'I can't believe it.'

He spent some time in the pinwheel of lights and music and tough guys and women from everywhere, including a Lufthansa flight attendant, a German blonde of striking figure. Somewhere in the night, Rosenthal had his head nestled on her large bosom.

'Abe, she wants to put you in an oven,' Fat Thomas said.

'I know,' Rosenthal said. 'I love it.'

I am home one Sunday morning when Peppy calls me. 'Right away,' he said. 'Major.'

I walk down to the bar, which was closed until 6 p.m. Peppy was pouring a big drink for a tired-looking guy who said he was the doorman at the Summit Hotel in Manhattan.

'Tell him,' Peppy said.

'Joe Namath come out in a fur coat 5 a.m. with Jill St John. He had a bottle.'

'That's it,' Peppy said. 'Don't tell me what broads and whiskey can do to a guy. We go naked.'

He told the doorman, 'Listen to me. Your car fare. Hear me? Bet your car fare. Namath goes home in an ambulance.'

The football game started at 1 p.m. in Shea Stadium, which sat freezing under a darkening winter sky. A wind screamed and spun inside the stadium.

Near the end of the game, Namath went toward the sideline at his own twelve and he threw the ball. Threw it through the wind and the darkness across the field and hit his end, Don Maynard, right on the hands. It was impossible that moment to think of anyone who was ever better.

Namath finished the day licking salt from his wrist and swallowing tequila on Third Avenue while a roomful of women crowded in.

Peppy sat at his bar in silence, his eyes closed, rubbing his forehead.

Another night I come up the subway steps glad to be home, because I had been working in the office on something for too long and it was almost midnight. I was going to turn to the right and our house when the neon pulled me to the left and into McGuire's. Only for a minute. I had too much illness at home to permit time for a saloon.

As I walked into the place, Jimmy Grant came over. His wife, Dell, the singer at Pep McGuire's, was Jimmy Burke's sister. Grant said, 'Jimmy has to talk to you right away. He's on the phone.' I went into the office and took the call. Jimmy Burke's voice boomed.

'You got to come down here,' he said. 'I got something for the cancer.'

'What is it?'

'Never mind. I got a way to get your wife cured. Come down. I'm at the Villagio.'

That was a restaurant on Rockaway Boulevard that was owned by Dominic Cataldo, who was a nice little guy but had a terrible reputation for doing a lot of work. The expression 'work' meant murder. This was a bad thing to say about Dominic, and, to make it worse, it was true.

I am faced with meeting Jimmy Burke and Dominic Cataldo alone on an empty sidewalk in the night. But why not? I know Jimmy a long time. He never would hurt me. Sure, I had written a lot about him running the Lufthansa robbery. That was business. How could I not write about a hold-up that big, six million? Did I put Burke right in the middle of it? I guess I did. At the same time, he and his crew were insanely shooting anybody who could link them to the heist. The police were going crazy with bodies.

I thought about a lawyer, Mike Coiro, who knew I had somebody sick at home. Maybe he told Jimmy something. And now Burke had something he thought could help me. Something out of the nights of nurses and hospitals and doctors and who knows. Only a week before, I was home watching a news show on Channel 13 where the head of the Red Cross, a doctor from the Anderson Cancer Center in Houston, and a scientist from Harvard, Dr Gilbert, were talking about a new treatment for cancer. A clinic in Sweden and another in Germany were reporting big news. The Red Cross man was exultant. 'There are exciting things happening in Sweden,' he said. 'Cures, not remissions. It is new and it is saving lives.'

I knew Gilbert, and so when the programme ended, I immediately called the television studio and asked the receptionist to get him for me. When he picked up, I told him I had to see him right away, and he said he was going to a lecture at New York Hospital on York Avenue. I got dressed, said nothing at home and took a cab to the lecture. On the way, I talked myself into putting the house up for sale in the morning, packing the family up and flying to Sweden.

I walked over to Gilbert, and he said, 'I couldn't talk to you on the phone because of all the people around me. I'm sorry you had to come all the way over here. But if you noticed, I didn't say anything while the man from the Red Cross made these outlandish claims. He is not even a doctor. He is a fund-raiser and he wants to excite donors. What he was talking about doesn't exist. His clinic in Sweden saves nobody. I'm sorry, but this has been almost a hoax tonight.'

Having gone through nights like that, and there were several, it still seemed only sensible to go down to see Burke. Little Dominic might be with him. I knew that lately he had been begging people to find him burial sites. But I could trust his waitress, Doris. She liked me, all right. And if I disappeared from the restaurant on this night, you could trust Doris to answer all police questions succinctly: 'Who?'

Nevertheless, we went down to the restaurant by cab.

Oh, yes, I was not alone. I was with my friend Victor Giuliani, who was a detective on the Queens burglary squad. I had asked him to come along with me and bring his gun.

As we were getting out of the cab, there was Jimmy Burke, alone, rumpled and loud.

'Why is he here?' he yelled, indicating Victor. 'I'm not going to kill you.'

Jimmy then walked up to us. 'I know Rose when you married her. The doctors know how to cure the disease. They won't do it unless they get paid. I got thirty-five thousand with me. I'll give it to you, and you give it to the doctor tomorrow, and he'll cure her. Don't worry about getting it back to me. I just want to see her cured. Just pay the doctor and let me know his name.'

I told him thanks but we were involved with a whole hospital full of doctors and so I'll pass. 'But I got to remember you for ever.'

Sometime later, Burke was convicted of fixing a Boston College basketball game. The college was the alma mater of the federal prosecutor in Brooklyn, Ed McDonald, who never stopped until Burke was sent away for a long time. Jimmy had left a mountain of bodies and the Lufthansa robbery, and they buried him on a missed lay-up. He came down with cancer in prison and died.

FOURTEEN

It is tempting to see the cops as the evil and bloodthirsty figures of this story, deserving of their fate, and Burt Kaplan as more sympathetic, less savage. But that would be wrong. What happened with Jeweller Number One, who was an honest thief, and Jeweller Number Two, who was also a thief but not so honest, is instructive as a look at how Burton Kaplan and his partners operated their business schemes. It is also important because it involves the first murder carried out by the Mafia Cops at Kaplan's direction. Rather than tell the tale myself, I let Burton Kaplan do the honour, since often he tells it better than even the greatest writer could.

Q: Mr Kaplan, in the mid-1980s, after you got out of Allenwood, did you get involved in a criminal scheme involving treasury bills?

A: Yes. The fellow who was taking these treasury bills worked in a depository place that held these bills and he would go through inventories every so often but right after an inventory came, he could take these bills and sell them to us, and if someone called up and tried to check if they were legitimate, they would come back legitimate.

Q: And who brought you this idea, this particular scheme?

A: Anthony Casso. He asked me if I could sell them, if I knew someone who could handle it and sell it. I said, Let me check it out, let me see what I could do. I called up Joe Banda, and I asked him to come and see me.

Q: Who was Joe Banda?

A: Joseph Banda was a jeweller who was a member of the Diamond Dealers Club, who was a partner of mine in a diamond deal that we had in Africa, and he was involved with me in many illegal deals.

Q: How had you met Banda?

A: I got involved in a diamond deal in Africa with an African fellow that was a friend of mine by the name of Mamadou Kwaitu. His uncle was in the administration in a country called Upper Volta and he became partners in a diamond mine in Central Africa called Bangi, and he gave his nephew Mamadou the right to sell the stones, the unpolished stones, the raw diamonds from this mine, if he was capable of selling it. And when the deal was offered to me, I asked Furnari if he knew anybody and he told me that a friend of his by the name of Frankie Hot – I don't know his last name, but he was in the diamond market downtown on Canal Street – and he said he would ask him, and then he made an appointment with me to go see Frankie Hot in the diamond market, and he introduced me to Joe Banda. Joe Banda and I had one-third apiece of the selling end of the diamonds from Africa.

Q: Where did Joe Banda live?

A: Williamsburg. Joe was a Hasidic Jew, and he wore the traditional clothing.

Q: OK. So when you approached Mr Banda with respect

to these treasury bills, can you tell the jury what you said to Mr Banda?

A: I told him that the bonds were still in the depository place and that I could get him numbers and pictures if he had the ability to sell them, and he said, I think I do, but give me the numbers of a couple and pictures and I'll get back to you.

Q: After giving him that information, did Banda indicate that he could fence those bills?

A: Yes. He said he had an associate of his that could sell them overseas. He was a jeweller. The guy had a bank, a banker, and that for a given amount of money the banker would cash, sell, the treasury bills for us, and we would get a dollar – if the treasury bill was worth a half million dollars, we would get a half million dollars, half of the money would go to Joe Banda, the banker and the jeweller, and the other half of the money would go to me and Casso and the people that supplied the treasury bills.

Q: And did there come a time that you went to Casso and actually obtained some of the bills?

A: I went to Casso and he wanted to give me two bills and I told him, Let's just try one, I don't want to be responsible for two. Let's just try one and see if it works.

Q: Did he give you one?

A: Yes, he did.

Q: And what happened with respect to that bill that he gave you?

A: I had met a fellow with Joe Banda in his car, and he asked me a lot of questions. He didn't see—

Q: I'm sorry, Mr Kaplan. Let me interrupt you. You have

the bill and you meet with, you say, a fellow named Joe, you met with Banda – and another man in a car?

A: Yes.

Q: Did you see this other man?

A: He was sitting in the front. The arrangements that I made with Banda, and Banda made with the gentleman, that he wouldn't look at me and I wouldn't look at him, so we could never identify each other.

Q: At some point in time, did Banda indicate to you where this other gentleman lived who was in the car?

A: I asked him, if we gave him the bill and the guy ran away, I wanted to know beforehand what the guy's name was and where he lived and where he worked. And the night I met the guy in the car, he wanted to give me that – Joe had told him that before – I said, No, just give it to Joe and Joe will give it to me if I need it. If the guy tried to rob the treasury bill from us.

Q: OK. Did you ever learn that man's name who you sat in the car with that day with Banda?

A: I had seen his name at one time, but I don't remember it.

Q: Did you refer to that man in some way?

A: Yes. That was Jeweller Number One. I don't know his name.

Q: What happens next with respect to this scheme?

A: I turned over the treasury bill to the gentleman with Joe Banda in the car that day. I gave him an envelope with the bill in it, and he proceeded to – he told me he was going overseas and he was going to cash the treasury bill and that they had a way that, once the money was free overseas, that they could make a phone call back here and that someone would have the money over here, so there was no trace of wires and things. It's common in the Hasidic community. The money never – the money never travels back and forth, it's just the percentages of interest for cashing it.

Q: So does there come a time that you receive some money from this deal?

A: Yes. Joe Banda gave me, about five or six, seven days later, he gave me about one hundred and thirty thousand, and a couple of days later he gave me one hundred and twenty thousand.

Q: And do you remember, Mr Kaplan, specifically the face value of the bonds or the bills you were dealing with?

A: Yes. That was half a million dollars. One bond, one treasury bill.

Q: So after you get the money from that, what happens? In the beginning, a few minutes ago, you mentioned that Casso had two bonds? And so what happens to that second bond?

A: I had told him, Go get me the other bond, and while we're doing the second bond, tell the guy that – to take a large amount of approximately ten million dollars and we'll do it all at one time now that we know it can go. These kind of deals don't continue, they open up, you do it and eventually the treasury bill will come back stolen, so let's do it and try and do ten million the next time. Casso told me he had given the treasury bill to someone else – just in case I couldn't complete the transaction, he would have another outfit – but he told me he told the guy, Just hold it, don't, don't do anything with it. And I asked Casso for the second treasury bill, and he said the guy told him that he would give it to him, and he never came back, and he asked him a second time, and the guy said, Listen, I gave it to a bank, a guy I know in a bank on Avenue U, and he tried to cash it, and the bill got confiscated.

Q: What did Casso say the name of the person was that he gave that bill to?

A: It was – it was a made member of the Lucchese crime family. I only knew him as Leo the Zip.

Q: With respect to Mr Leo, did anything happen to him?

A: Yes. Casso got very aggravated, because he now had the opportunity to sell ten million dollars' worth of treasury bills, and Casso had him murdered.

Q: And can you tell the jury, did you become aware of certain questioning that was taking place regarding this bond deal? And how did you become aware of that?

A: Joe Banda came to me and he said, We have a problem. I said, What's the problem? He said, The banker is being questioned by Interpol. I said, What's the problem? He got a hundred thousand dollars for doing this. Why should he have a problem misleading them? And he said he just found out, Joe told me he just found out. 'Til today I question that the banker never got the money, that the guy who said he was – who eventually became Jeweller Number Two never gave the banker the hundred thousand and therefore the banker had every right in the world to give the authorities the information.

Q: There was some indications that you had that there was law-enforcement interest because of the bonds getting some attention as being illegal?

A: Yes.

Q: OK. You described a meeting in a car before with a jeweller. You gave him a number. What jeweller number was that?

A: That was Jeweller Number One.

Q: OK. Does he ever get killed, Jeweller Number One?

A: No.

Q: In discussions with the government, did you tell us that person's name?

A: I didn't know his name. I learned it and I forgot it.

Q: OK. How did you refer to him in discussions with the government?

A: The one I met in the car was Jeweller Number One. The jeweller that – that had the banking connection was Jeweller Number Two.

Q: Is Jeweller Number Two a person who you eventually give a murder contract to kill?

A: Yes.

'Eventually' meaning not just yet. In fact, there was another scheme, not so different from the one involving bonds, that sealed Jeweller Number Two's fate.

Q: Can you tell the jury who Tommy Carmada is?

A: He was an associate of a fellow by the name of Frank Buschemi, who was a friend of mine, and he was a guy that always came up with schemes. He worked for a company that installed safes for businesses and people's homes, and he was what we would call a tipster, gave people information and places to rob, and he had a connection in a place, a brokerage house where cheques were being mailed to people.

Q: Did he bring a scheme involving those cheques to you? A criminal scheme?

A: Yes. Carmada told me that the person that he has in the brokerage house gets the cheques about two weeks before they are to be mailed to the individual people or corporations, and he said at that point he can get the cheques two weeks before the people would normally expect them in the mail, and he could give them to me if I had a connection to fence the cheques, to cash them.

Q: And as to when the cheques came out of the place where they were, were they – you said they were hot. Can you just explain the distinction there?

A: Yeah, they were definitely stolen cheques.

Q: But were they—

A: They were not hot at that point because—

Q: Explain that.

A: Because the people that were going to get them, receive them, didn't expect them two weeks before time, so nobody would be looking for them. They would be just normal good cheques. He asked me if I could fence them.

Q: What did you tell him?

A: I called up Joe Banda.

Q: Is that the same Banda that was involved in the treasury-bill deal with you?

A: Yes.

Q: Was the treasury-bill deal first or this cheque deal first?

A: The treasury bills.

Q: How much time between the treasury-bill deal and the cheque deal, if you could approximate?

A: Probably four years – '85.

Q: What did you say to Mr Banda?

A: I told him the situation exactly as it was explained to me by Tommy Carmada, that I could get these cheques two weeks before people expected them, and if he had a connection to deposit them the same way he did with the treasury bills, we could get the cheques and have them cashed and get the money before the people would ever expect them in the mail.

Q: What did Banda say to you?

A: He says he has the same connection with Jeweller Number One and that he would go and speak to him and get back to me.

Q: Explain what you mean by the same connection with Jeweller Number One.

A: They could cash it, and we would receive the money the same way as we received the treasury-bill money, without any wires.

Q: This Jeweller Number One, was he the person that had come to the meeting with you in the car with Banda?

A: Yes.

Q: So he was not killed in the bond deal?

A: No.

Q: Given what happened in the bond deal, why was it that you were willing to work with Jeweller Number One again?

A: Because Joe Banda explained to me that he and Jeweller Number One lived up to their end of the bargain, that Jeweller Number Two was the one who put the money in his pocket and never gave it back.

Joe Banda assured me that Jeweller Number One was a credible person.

Q: Did there come a time that you received the cheques from Carmada and gave them to Banda?

A: Yes. I gave the cheques to Joe Banda and he gave them to Jeweller Number One, who flew overseas and deposited the cheques.

Q: Did you see him give those to Jeweller Number One or did Banda tell you something about that?

A: I didn't see him give the cheques to Jeweller Number One, but I met Jeweller Number One, and I handed him the first treasury bill myself, and I – Joe Banda told me, I'm giving these cheques to Jeweller Number One, and I assumed that he did.

Q: Did Banda use the term 'Jeweller Number One'?

A: No. He says, I'm giving it to my friend who you met in the car.

Q: So after you gave the cheques to Banda, can you tell the jury what was the next significant thing that happened regarding this cheque deal?

A: We waited four, five, six days, which was the normal period of time that Joe said it would take, and then Carmada started asking for the money on the cheques. I went to see Joe, and I said to Joe, What's going on with the cheques? He says, Well, we didn't get any money yet, maybe it's going to take another couple of days. And then another couple of days went by, and I said to Joe, What's going on with the cheques? And he was a little evasive, and then he said, I think there's a problem, I think that the cheques were confiscated and that they were hot cheques. They were not – they were not imported already, and the bank never cleared the cheques and confiscated them, and I have a feeling that the government is talking to Jeweller Number One.

Q: Banda told you that?

A: Yes.

Q: When he said 'the government is talking to Jeweller Number One', can you just explain what that means to the jury?

A: The government was investigating the stolen cheques, and they came back during the investigation to Jeweller Number One, and they were speaking to him.

Q: That's what Banda told you?

A: Yes.

Q: Can you tell the jury what the phrase 'stand up' means, or 'he stood up' – what's that mean in your life?

A: Stand-up is what I used to be. When someone has a problem, they take their punishment and go to jail, they don't give up anybody. They take – they take responsibility for the crime.

Q: So didn't Jeweller Number One stand up previously?

A: Yes.

Q: So what made you believe that he wasn't going to stand up this time?

A: Joe Banda led me to believe that.

Q: Did Banda know at that point in time what you had done to Jeweller Number Two?

A: He didn't know.

We make one important editorial comment here. The career of a criminal, just like that of a politician, often has years pass between noteworthy events. A state assemblyman may sit quietly through two or three terms before he thinks of something that makes even the least bit of sense. The criminal of course can be off the grid for five, ten and these days even twenty years. The other profession where years frequently are lost is boxing. *The Ring Record Book* runs an annual list of a fighter's bouts, and here and there it states: '2002–2005 INACTIVE'. During that span, the fighter was probably quite active at recreation periods in San Quentin but missing at Olympia Auditorium matches.

Q: After Banda told you about his concerns regarding Jeweller Number One, what did you do next?

A: I told him the same thing as I told him on the other jeweller: Get me all the information on him – his name, where he lives, where he works, what kind of car he drives – and I said, You have that already once before from the guy. He said, I don't really remember where I put it, but I'll get it for you by tomorrow.

Q: Did Banda ever indicate to you that he knew Jeweller Number One?

A: Yes, he definitely knew him. He lived in the same neighbourhood as Joe, in Williamsburg.

Q: OK. So I will take you to the time where you first learned of the law-enforcement attention with respect to this bond deal. What happened after you learned of that law-enforcement attention?

A: I asked Joe Banda – I asked Joe what was going on. He told me that – that the banker was being questioned by Interpol and that he was told Jeweller Number Two was going to tell them that he got the bonds – the treasury bill from Joe Banda. I said to Joe, I don't understand what's going on. The banker got a hundred thousand and I didn't even know there was a Jeweller Number Two. I thought Jeweller Number One had the connection with the bank. He said no, there was another jeweller. So I said, Did the banker get the hundred thousand? He says, No. I said, you know, Then what happened? He says, I thought the second jeweller was giving him the money. He deducted it from the cut-up. But he never gave him the money. Then I – I made up my mind that if Jeweller Number Two lied and said he gave the banker the hundred thousand and put the hundred thousand in his pocket, he was a guy that was going to give up Joe Banda, and then Joe Banda was going to give me up, and I would go back to prison, and I put a contract out on the guy. On Jeweller Number Two.

Q: OK. So Jeweller Number Two is the one who actually has the connections in Europe, is that correct?

A: Yes. Joe Banda comes and tells me. He said that the banker was being bothered and that the banker called Jeweller Number Two – and was telling him that the government was looking – was looking to investigate this, this crime, and Joe told me that he felt that Jeweller Number Two was going to cooperate. Joe would get implicated, and I felt then that I would get implicated.

Q: What if anything did you ask Banda to do?

A: I asked Banda to get me the – the Jeweller Number Two's home address, where he worked, what kind of car he drove, the licence-plate number.

Q: About how much time went by before he gave it to you?

A: Very quickly, within a couple of days.

Q: What did you tell Banda you needed the information for?

A: I told him that we were going to – to talk to the guy and try and shake him up, try and get him to – to go back to the point where he won't cooperate.

Q: When you say 'shake him up,' what do you mean by that?

A: Scare him, threaten him.

Q: In terms of scaring him or threatening him, what specifically do you mean? Do you mean to have him beaten up?

A: No. Just to grab him and show him that we could grab him and tell him that he took money to do what he did. He was a partner in this thing, and he was the one who was the liar. If he had given the banker the hundred thousand, there wouldn't have been a problem. The banker probably would have went along with the scheme. That's what I told Joe.

Q: OK. Did Banda, in your estimate, have any other indications from you that you were going to have this guy killed?

A: No. I called up Frank Santora.

Q: All right. After you contacted Santora, did there come a time that you had a conversation with him about this?

A: I told him I had a problem and I felt it was going to be a very serious problem, and I asked him if he had the ability to – to take a murder contract.

Q: What did he say to you?

A: Without any doubt. He said he was going to go and see his cousin and talk it over with his cousin. Frankie said there was no problem. It could be handled.

Q: OK. What happened next?

A: I had – Frankie came back and told me that they could do it and give him whatever information I have on the guy, and we discussed money.

Q: When Frankie said to you they could do it, what did you take that to mean?

A: Meaning him and his cousin and whoever else they were going to use at that point. I didn't know Steve at that point. When we agreed on the price, Frankie told me it was him, his cousin and his cousin's partner.

Q: OK. For the record, did you later learn who Frankie's cousin was that he was referring to?

A: Louis Eppolito.

Q: Who was the cousin's partner that Santora was referring to?

A: Stephen Caracappa.

Q: OK. So when you discussed price for the murder of Jeweller Number Two, what was – what were the discussions?

A: I told him I had – didn't have a lot of money at that particular time and – but he knew I was good for it and I said, Would you take twenty-five thousand dollars for this? I could pay it ten, ten and five, every week. And Frankie said, That's fair. Don't worry about it. And he – he took the contract.

Q: So what was the agreement, the essence of the agreement between you and the other parties?

A: That I would pay him twenty-five thousand dollars and that he and his associates, Frank Santora's cousin and Frank Santora's cousin's partner, would kill the jeweller.

Q: Did you have any discussions with Mr Santora about the plan for carrying out the murder?

A: That they would find out where he – check his address, check his house, and check where he worked and take him as he was coming down the – the highway, the roads coming from his house to work. They would pull him over with a flashing light. And they told me that they would say that he was wanted for a hit-and-run and that someone wanted to look at him, and if it wasn't him, they would take him back right away. And they got in – in the car. The jeweller got in the car, according to Frankie, with Steve and Louie, and Frankie drove the jeweller's car.

Q: OK. So you went from Santora telling you about how it was going to be carried out to when Santora told you about what actually happened?

A: How it was done. Next thing that happened is I got called to a – to a business meeting in Arizona, and I went to Arizona. Frank called my house, and I called my wife and said, Tell him I'll be home in two days, but if it is an emergency, give him the number where I'm staying and have him call me. She says, He said he'll see you when you get back.

Q: Prior to meeting with Santora when you got back from Arizona, did you have a phone conversation with him in order to arrange the meeting?

A: Yes. He told me that he was going to come and see me.

Q: When you met with Santora, what did he tell you about what had happened?

A: Yes. That they – the guy was driving his car and they pulled him over. The three of them were in one car. Frank, Louie and Steve. And that they put on the flashing light and they pulled the guy over and they told him that he was wanted in a hit-and-run and that they had to take him in for a line-up and that if he wasn't identified, they would take him right back. And they put him in the car, and then Frankie got in his car. They took him to a – according to Frankie, they took him to a – to an automobile-repair place or collision place that was a friend of theirs, and I said to Frankie, What happened? He says, We shot him. I said, Who shot him? He says, I did. I said, Then what happened to him? He said, I took him out and I got rid of the body. I said, Does – does the other two guys know where the body is? He says, No. He says, I wouldn't trust anybody with that information.

Q: In your experience in organised crime, is it common or uncommon to be told where a body is buried?

A: Uncommon. Because some days people – later on in life people become informants and they would be able to lead people to the body, government people to the body.

Q: Did Santora tell you anything about what he did with Jeweller Number Two's car?

A: Yes. He told me he took it to the airport. He put it in long-term parking, and he left it there.

Q: After Santora told you about what had been done, did there come a time that you paid Santora?

A: Yes. A total of thirty thousand dollars.

Q: As a part of your cooperation agreement on this case, did you plead guilty to this murder?

A: Yes.

Q: At the time you pled guilty to this murder, did you know the person's name who was murdered?

A: No.

Q: Do you know it as you sit here today?

A: No.

Q: Did you ever get questioned by Mr Banda about what had happened?

A: Yes. I told him the jeweller must have ran away. He
        must have ran away from the government, from the
        investigation. Must have run out on a long vacation.

'They come in here, fifty of them,' Dominick from Kiev is saying.

He is standing at the entrance to the parking lot and collision garage at 2232 Nostrand Avenue in Brooklyn.

'Who?'

'All agents, police, who knew? They wouldn't say anything to me. They stood here and talked. About nothing. They do nothing. They stand here and talk. Fifty of them, they stand here talking about nothing.'

Dominick is describing the platoon of federal agents who rushed to this place upon Burton Kaplan's courtroom discourse concerning the unhappy fate of Jeweller Number Two.

'Then come all the televisions. I stood inside the office from them. I still saw me on television. They got it from the helicopter.'

Burt Kaplan testified that this lot was where Lou Eppolito and Steve Caracappa took the jeweller and murdered him on a cold morning.

'We have organised crime in Kiev where I come from,' Dominick says, 'but the government is the boss, the top people, so they do not come and take your parking to bury somebody. Why should they? They have all of Russia to bury anybody they kill. The government has some reason they do not tell you for killing a person. Here, the organised crime must shut somebody's mouth. They know. Organised crime here has a reason. We don't know anything in Kiev. Here is better. At least some of us know.'

The entrance to the lot is narrow and has a chain-link gate. On the right is a small hut with a peaked roof and windows, which give a clear view of parked cars. This is the office, where bills are noted and a dispatcher directs the tow trucks. You walk inside the gate to a row of stubby garages, sixteen of them. They face a line of delivery vans and contractors' panel trucks nosed against a storm fence, which runs along a muddy bank that spills twenty feet down a slope to old railroad tracks. They are covered with so much garbage that only a few yards of track can be seen.

Dominick from Kiev works for the lot's owner, Peter Franzone, fifty-six, 5 ft 4 in. Franzone had told police, 'I saw three men go into garage number four and only two come out.'

Franzone has his own story. He was nine years old and working at a grocery store after school. He and a couple of other kids broke into a recycling plant. The score was sixty-five dollars. Young Franzone went on rides at Coney Island and ate hot dogs and bought a cowboy hat and a toy gun. Pete and friends were caught two days later. The cowboy hat got him off. Then he becomes old enough to do man's work, age twelve, in a junkyard. He makes eight dollars a week and he gives most of it to his mother. He keeps a couple of dollars in order to be a big guy in the candy store. This starts a life in which he did not miss a day of work. He drove a Chinese laundry truck when he was under-age, fixed flats at a gas station, worked in junkyards, which creates too much familiarity with cars that belong to others. He is driving with his friends in a car that does not belong to him. The ride ends as quickly as it starts. Franzone had an accident, and the cops took him to a judge who, discovering that the urchin in the well could not read, sent him to an upstate youth facility that Peter remembers as a farm with classrooms. He evaded reading and writing lessons by studying welding. He went back to the junkyard, where he took radiators and starters out of the smashed cars, cleaned the parts up and sold them as second-hand. He did this until he was twenty-one and could get a tow-truck driver's licence. You tell me how he got a tow-truck driver's licence without being able to read.

He left the sixth grade at age sixteen unable to read, but he could make out some letters. Over the years, he deciphered T-O-W, which was good enough. By now he owned two tow trucks, which he kept in his collision garage next to his parking lot. His wife was not only literate but efficient: she filled out and mailed promptly the bills for having your vehicle towed.

Somebody always hangs out at a collision shop. With Franzone it was a guy named Frank Santora who was around in 1978 or so. Santora had an Oldsmobile that was damaged and asked Franzone to work on it. He came around three or four times a week and rode tow-truck days with Franzone. He let Franzone pay for lunch. He said he was a salesman, but when Franzone asked what he sold, he talked about good barbers for his hair, which he was proud of. He was around for years, and when Franzone moved to the Nostrand Avenue lot, Santora came with the sale.

Late one afternoon in the mid-'80s, Santora told Franzone that he wanted him to meet his cousin Lou Eppolito. Santora introduced him as a cop in the Sixty-third Precinct. Eppolito was alone with his gold chains and jewellery in a car parked at the kerb, on Nostrand Avenue. He came around like this several times.

It only followed that one afternoon Eppolito pulled in to the parking lot and went down a few spaces and backed the car into a space along the fence. It only followed because these rodents scratch their way into somebody's life, into your building, your car, your business, anything that isn't theirs, and then they declare that they are in. And so Louie Eppolito sits in his car. Yes, I am here whether you want me or not. And now you are part of this whether you want it or not. There is a sudden blur in the corner of Franzone's eye: three people walking into the lot. One was Santora. Alongside him, in beard and yarmulke, was Israel Greenwald, Jeweller Number Two in Burt Kaplan's testimony. On the other side of Greenwald was a guy with a trench-coat collar covering one side of his face. Franzone said he had the coat buttoned 'like when you see in movies, like when you're watching their movies, they always have the guy with the lapels that go up around his ears'. Franzone made him as Caracappa.

The three walked shoulder to shoulder to garage number four. Franzone watched as Santora closed the door and then in a little while walked out with the trench coat to the front gate. Where's the third guy?

He found out. Santora called him in. The third guy was dead

against the wall inside the garage. Pete Franzone was told to start digging a hole in the garage floor.

'Just dig, or we'll kill you and your family,' Franzone says Santora told him.

Franzone glanced around as he threw dirt and saw the seated Greenwald. He must be dead because he is not breathing. I will not be next. Pete Franzone dug for his life in the hard dirt. He was a couple of feet down in the garage floor. He got the hole down to about the required six feet and then he and Santora threw the body of Israel Greenwald into the hole. That is the last time he does business with us, Santora said to himself. Santora brought in cement, lime and water from his trunk. The garage was baptised with its first mob death.

The next time he saw Louie Eppolito drive into the lot, Franzone tried to flee. But then came Santora in a white Cadillac. He parked at the entrance to the collision shop and summoned Franzone. Santora opened the car trunk. It was empty. Pete saw this as a prelude to something ugly. The trunk was empty so there would be room for something later on.

Santora said he would be joined by some other people. Franzone went to his hut in hopes he would be forgotten during the meeting. Santora called him from the collision shop. 'It is too hot here,' Santora said. 'You have to come over and turn off the heat.' Pete went to the shop, pulled a switch and kept his eyes on the ceiling and thus away from anything frightful. As he started to leave, a hand came up to stop him. 'He was like on his knees wrapping a body up,' Franzone says. 'He says, "You have to help me get this thing into the trunk."' Pete didn't want to know the guy's name. He was wrapping the body like a butcher would tie a roast. He had it inside a blanket, and he threaded the rope over and tied it and then under and moved down the package and kept tying.

Then the guy yelped that Franzone had touched the packaged body without wearing gloves. 'You left fingerprints! You could bury us.' The guy kept muttering as he wiped the blanket.

They gave Franzone gloves, and he helped stuff the body into the trunk of Santora's car. Finally Franzone was able to get out and he left, but he knew it would never end.

Later, when he was asked if he had called police or any federal agencies, he said, 'Never, because you know they would probably call up Louie Eppolito and say I got a nut here saying you killed somebody and this, that and the other, and I figured that he'll come and get me and kill me or lock me up and have somebody in jail kill me. Then they would kill my family.'

Franzone despised what he had been forced to do. Later, when his son was born, Frank Santora brought around baby clothes in a garbage bag. He came with his wife and daughter. Look what we brought you, isn't this sweet? The clothes still had tags on them. Franzone acted grateful. Then Santora left and Franzone threw the clothes out. 'I didn't want my son to wear anything from Frankie Santora.'

FIFTEEN

She didn't know who he was, and therefore we cannot give her credit for extraordinary courage; and besides, she was only following her heritage of thievery.

Her driver pulled up at Park Avenue and Fifty-ninth Street, and she was out and running right at Tony Café, who is standing on the corner with a cane because he has just had a knee operation. He is scouring the traffic for his ride.

'Poppy!' she called through the Christmas crowd. 'Oh, my Poppy, Poppy.'

The gypsy was on him before he knew she was there.

'Oh, Poppy. How's my Poppy?' A scarf covered half of her face and she kept her head down. Right away she tapped his bad leg.

All of a sudden she is touching his shirt inside his jacket. 'How is it coming along? Oh, Poppy, you just get better.'

For one second he made her for a nurse, because just last week he had been in the big hospital down at the end of the block. All the nurses loved him. How could you not like Tony Café? Everybody knew who he was.

Hey, now what is this? Hands all over him. He steps back.

'Good-bye, Poppy. You get better.'

She was in the car and gone.

Tony Café went for his wallet. It was still there. He looked inside. The money was there. I guess she was a nurse. Now he put his

155

hand in his pants pocket for his roll. Which was gone. Four hundred eighty-five dollars.

'She beat me. She is a fucking gypsy, and she beats me out of four hundred and eighty-five dollars.' How could such a thing happen to the boss of a Mafia family from Brooklyn? For a girl to dip him is past anything we even imagined. It is the end of the year 2006. They are mugging Mafia bosses on the street.

'I just gave him a cheque for fifty thousand,' Tony Café is telling me the last time I saw him, a couple weeks after he got mugged. He indicates the lawyer, David Breitbart, who is walking ahead of him up the steps of the Queens County Criminal Court on Queens Boulevard, New York City.

'What did he say?'

'He said, "Oh, you kept your word." What does he think I do, not live up to it? He asked me for seventy-five and I said I'd have fifty today. That's what I have.'

'How much more do you owe him?'

'He is doing the case for three hundred thousand. He knows I looked around. Lefcourt wanted seven-fifty. Goldberg wanted four hundred. I thought Breitbart would be the best. He handled our people before and he knows us.'

'Our people' means the Bonanno family, one of the five outfits that once ruled the streets and now fill courtrooms. For years, Tony had been mostly, happily, invisible. I looked at these Mafia charts that prosecutors put up on courtroom easels for the benefit of juries, and I never once saw Tony's face there. I never read his name in the papers either. Good boy, Tony Café.

Then, in 1982, Joe Massino of the Bonanno family gets indicted along with about fifty others for murder, robbery and obstruction of justice. And Anthony Rabito, aka Tony Café, rises from blessed obscurity to a spot on a stage that has suddenly exploded into hot white light beaming all over him.

There was a knock on the door one day. Somebody is down on the street banging, and Tony is upstairs in his house in Greenpoint, Brooklyn, with his 88-year-old sister, with whom he lives. He looks out the window. There are three lawmen there, but two are on the front stoop and he can't see them. One agent steps out onto the sidewalk so Tony can see.

'FBI!'

'Yeah, so?'

'We want to talk to you.'

Now the other two come on the sidewalk. One is a female agent named McCaffrey. Typical FBI, an Irish woman sent to humiliate an Italian.

'I'll be right there,' Tony said.

He gives his wallet to his sister, in case he isn't coming back. He goes downstairs.

'Are you arresting me?'

'No.'

'Then what do you want me for? I live upstairs with my sister. Eighty-year-old woman sick with cancer. There are no guns or money in the house. I have to call my lawyer.'

Tony remembers the Irish woman telling him, 'You're number one now. We don't want any bodies in the street. We don't want witnesses intimidated. We don't want agents threatened. You're number one. You make sure.'

Later, as he walks the streets of Greenpoint, which now is virtually a desert, he tells himself in wonderment, 'I'm a boss!'

They came back a couple of weeks later. Tony remembers the male agent saying, 'Could you do us a favour?'

'We always did little favours for the FBI,' Tony recalls. 'Nobody gets hurt if we help them. They help us back. So the agent says, "We can't have any bodies around. It'll cause us a lot of trouble with our bosses. Could you do us a favour and tell them all, Don't have any murders?"

'At this time,' Tony is saying, 'there were only two people who were doing that kind of work.' He made a gun out of his hand. 'I had to go out and find them or get somebody to find them and tell them, "Don't do nothing."'

The law next came on a Sunday morning, banging on the door and calling on the phone at the same time. When he answered the phone, a city detective outside yelled, 'Open the door!' He did and was arrested. They led him out of the house. The FBI did not exactly renege after he had helped them. The woman, McCaffrey, was there writing down notes, but it was an arrest by city detectives on a Queens County bookmaking charge having nothing to do with the federal government. He was in a week until he was released on million-dollar bail, for which he posted two houses in Greenpoint, including the one where he lives. He does have a woman friend in Manhattan, someone of appropriate age for Tony, now in his early seventies.

We pick up Tony Café and his lawyer going into court on that bookmaking charge. It should be nothing too serious, except that his role as the new leader of the Bonanno family makes even a gambling offence insurmountable. On this case he was charged with running a web of twenty-two cell phones for a large bookmaking and loan-sharking business in Brooklyn and Queens. He was an old target, with straw sticking out from earlier government arrows, but still a target.

The others arrested with him on this day were seven men over seventy. Three others in their late sixties were all seriously ill with ailments of the aged. There can be no surer enforcement against the Mafia than a stopped heartbeat. Sal Scudiero, seventy-two, charged with being the gunman, was too weak to stand in court.

Tony's past was right across Queens Boulevard from the courthouse. The lights at Pep McGuire's bar always shrieked in the night for Tony Café, who spilled out of his car with a huge smile and plunged into the place. He was named Tony Café by Pep himself because that was the only place you ever saw Tony, in a café. Pep and Johnny McGuire threw Tony Café at as many women as they could, and he beamed and drank and exploded with joy.

Tony rolled through these nights thirty years ago with a whole mob and, for a time, their new heavy hitter, a tough guy named Donnie Brasco.

When last seen, Brasco was taking the witness stand in Room 103, federal court, Manhattan. Tony Café and others of the Bonanno crew sat with lawyers.

Q: What is your name?

A: Joseph Pistone.

Q: What is your occupation?

A: I am a special agent of the Federal Bureau of Investigation.

There are times when the expression 'the roof caves in' has a certain validity. Sitting in the back row on this day, and lucky to be there, Fat Thomas took a huge breath. 'I am having a cardiac arrested.'

Tony Café was sentenced to eight years. He told the judge that he had fought two years in Korea, that both his brothers had served there, too, and that he deserved something for this. The judge took two years off the sentence. Tony did six years at Otisville federal prison in upstate New York. He happened not to like it. As I said, I didn't see him when he came out and never heard about him again, so I figured he wasn't up to much, which was good, because thanks to RICO a second sentence would run him a thousand years.

But now, instead of having a dance floor under his feet, Tony Café is on the wrong side of Queens Boulevard. He trudges up the cement courthouse steps and goes into a large courtroom with low lights. The defendants, while seated, look like they should be waiting on a bench outside a supermarket pharmacy window somewhere in Florida.

When the case is called, the lawyers stand in front and the defendants wait two rows behind them. The purpose of the appearance is to make sure everybody has a lawyer and that all tapes and photos and other evidence are made available to the defence by the assistant district attorney, a Ms Kane.

One of the old men calls out, 'I don't want a lawyer.' Another one, in a blue shirt, is asked, 'Do you have a lawyer?' He does not reply or even move. Somebody says, 'He can't hear.' A court officer talks directly into the man's ear. He says something back. 'He is going to get a lawyer,' the court officer announces.

Alexander Noce, seventy-two, told his lawyer, Mathew Mari, 'I can't afford nothing. Make sure I don't have to pay nothing.'

The prosecutor now mentioned fifty thousand dollars bail. Mari spoke out immediately to the judge. 'Your Honour, my client can't tie up that much money. For a very good reason. He won't be able to feed his family.'

The judge lowered it to twenty-five thousand dollars.

'Your Honour, thank you,' Mari said.

'What did he do?' the client, Noce, said.

'He cut it to twenty-five thousand dollars.'

Noce groaned loudly.

Mari clasped his hands in prayer and held them at Noce's face. 'Shut up or I'll ask the judge to remand you. You don't deserve a lawyer like me.' Another date is set for a hearing on evidence, and all the old men shuffle out of the room.

The combined cost of lawyers figures to be about a million dollars.

The defendants go from Queens Boulevard to Withers Street in Greenpoint, in Brooklyn, a short, narrow block off an expressway that rises to the Williamsburg Bridge, which crosses the East River to downtown Manhattan. On one side of Withers Street are three-storey stone houses where families have lived for years. There used to be a piano teacher there who rented her kitchen and phone to bookmakers working for James 'Jimmy Nap' Napoli. He, too, was in education: he sponsored a college scholarship fund for the children of friendly police officers. Among the neighbourhood children taking music lessons there was Arlene D'Arienzo. The piano was in the living room, she remembers. The bookmakers on the phones in the kitchen kept pleading, 'We can't hear nothing. How long does she have to go?'

On the other side of the street is Bamonte's, with the longevity of a pyramid. The men from court walk into the afternoon dimness of the restaurant. Their leader, Tony Café, tells the waiter, 'We're not going to eat. We may eat later. Right now we're just holding court.'

All sit at a large round table. Their worries are about the aftermaths of heart surgeries and, simultaneously, the criminal charges traditionally reserved for young Mafia racketeers. Tony Café nods at the others.

'They took away our Social Security,' Vinny, seventy-one, says.

'They stopped all our Social Security,' Salvatore, seventy-three, says.

'They can't do that. Not on a gambling charge,' someone says. 'Only when you're convicted.'

'I get Social Security eight hundred a month,' Georgie says. 'If I don't get that, I live in the street. My daughter gets four hundred a month. If they ever take that away from her . . .'

'They can't stop your daughter's cheque,' one of them says.

'Can't,' Frank says.

'They can do anything they fucking want,' Al says.

'They stopped my Social Security and VA benefits,' Tony Café says.

'He was in Korea in the army and they take away his VA benefits. How can they do that?' Georgie says.

'I get altogether two thousand a month,' Tony Café says. 'That's what I live on. How can they take my VA?'

'I stood next to you when we were getting sentenced,' Red says to Tony Café. 'They asked you if you wanted to say something, You said, "I was in the army in Korea for this country. I love the flag. I love everybody."'

Tony says, 'The judge took two years off what he was going to give me. I only had to do six.'

'I'm standing next to you,' Red says. 'I tell myself, "This is going to be all right." Then he gave me twenty years.'

'Do you know between us we have four open-heart surgeries?' Frankie from Staten Island says. 'How do you like it? A big police raid and they get four guys over seventy who had open-heart surgery. You call us threats?'

'Four open hearts,' another says.

'They got diabetes. Blood sugar,' Anthony says.

'I got two broken toes,' Tony Café says. 'The doctor says it's from diabetes. What am I going to do in jail?'

'You think they care?' Salvatore from the neighbourhood says. 'When they came in on me, the one held a gun right to my head and another gun right in my side.'

'Why?'

'I had a gun in the house. It had dust on it. They said if I moved, they'd blow my head off. Move? I can hardly take a breath.'

'When they arraigned us,' Sal says, 'one of the agents said, "Cover the back door so he don't try to run out." The judge said, "Run out? He can't walk."'

'They spent more time writing down the medicine we had to have,' Vinny says.

Now the men have gone home for afternoon naps or early dinner, and Tony Café sits alone at the bar.

Bamonte's appears to be an out-of-the-way place, but it is on Broadway in the world of New York people who know what they are eating. It is a short drive from Manhattan, and at lunchtime half the city seems to walk past the bar to the dining room. Police Commissioner Ray Kelly came often, shaking hands with everybody he saw. Once Tony Café held out his hand, and Kelly grabbed it and then moved on.

Today, in the gloaming, Tony Café sits at the empty restaurant and says, 'The police commissioner shook my hand. How do you like it? He didn't know who I was. Nobody knows who I am. I don't know anybody else. They're all in jail. Once the top of the family turns, like Joe Massino did, then nobody from the other families will talk to you.'

'What was the worst thing to happen to the outfit?' he is asked.

'Gotti,' he says slowly. 'When he had the case against him with a woman prosecutor and he fixed the jury. That got the government mad. Nobody was safe after that. They got Gotti, and then they came after everybody else. Because of him, all of a sudden I'm standing out here alone.'

SIXTEEN

In my years in the newspaper business, the Mafia comes down to one thing: circulation. On the Sunday in 1985 that John Gotti started his famous swagger through the city and onto every TV screen in America, the *New York Daily News* sold 1.8 million papers. After so many years of photos and headlines and suits and ties and haircuts and murders, after all of it, Gotti is dead. His son Junior just spent time in prison and on trial three times in this same twenty-sixth floor federal courtroom in Manhattan. He doesn't sell forty papers. The *News* on Sunday now has a circulation of seven hundred and seventy thousand and falling. The worst thing you can say about a Gotti is that he doesn't sell papers.

'I am proud that my son got made,' John Gotti one day announced to Vincent Gigante.

'I'm sorry to hear that,' Gigante said. Sometimes in nepotism you get nepotted.

The Mafia was already in decline when Gotti arrived. The way I knew it was to listen or walk the streets. The crime family named for the late Carlo Gambino, a slight, scheming man, was taken over at his death by his cousin Paul Castellano. He lasted little. Gotti had him shot to death. Fame by pistol. The old man of the Gambino crew, Joe N.

Gallo told Gotti, 'It took a hundred years to put this together and you're ruining it in six months.'

He appears to have been right. This old organisation started in Naples and Reggio Calabria and the narrow, wet alleys of Palermo. Hungry young men came by packed ships to the streets of the Lower East Side of New York. Their names were Joe the Boss and Lupo the Wolf and Lucky Luciano. Soon their children were growing up ferociously on crowded cement. Their murderous, larcenous hands reached everywhere. They swore one another to secrecy.

In a trial in Brooklyn, the judge asked the defendants to stand when their names were called so the jury would know them. Gotti rose, a Roman conqueror, and with a small, pleasant smile, half nodded and half bowed to the jury, Look at me, I am humbling myself before you, you fucking commoners.

In his home club, the Bergin Hunt and Fish, coming in to start the day at eleven, Gotti looked at the newspapers on a table and if his name or picture wasn't in any of them, there was no living with him. He would stomp into the rear room and sit in a barber chair and bellow. He made a bright day miserable.

These imbeciles got so excited when they saw themselves on television or their pictures in the paper that they could barely breathe. There was no significant trend in organised crime that you had to be brilliantly perceptive to see. All you had to do was let a mafioso read a newspaper each day and give him time to watch the six o'clock news, and the whole thing would come crashing down on its own.

As gangsters did not have the legs to remain standing on street corners all day, and most certainly could not sit at home or their families would flee, they opened their own social clubs. There these men could sit and do nothing, at which they were excellent. Carmine Lombardozzi had a clubhouse on Seventy-fifth Street in Brooklyn. Greg Scarpa and Carmine Persico were on Eighty-fifth and Eleventh. Anthony Spero was around on Bath Avenue. Some blocks to the west were the clubs of John Gotti, including the Café Liberty, under the Liberty Avenue el on Eighty-fourth Street, where there were so many known bugs in the walls and ceiling that all members were ordered not to talk but instead to write notes to each other. Peter Gotti tried, but soon his hand pained him. He also realised that the notes were useless because his friend Skinny Dom Pizzonia couldn't read. Peter began talking again. Skinny Dom welcomed the sound and talked back. Soon there were so many wiretap tapes of them that the courtroom needed a disc jockey.

All the tough guys, Skinny Dom and Fat Andy and Sal Reale and Peter Gotti, sat in the Liberty club and strangled time. The doors and windows were sealed, and since all inside smoked, one after the other, the place was a fog-bank.

There was a round table where everybody sat on folded metal chairs and choked side by side.

'We ought to stop smoking,' Reale said.

'No,' everybody answered.

'We get an air conditioner,' Reale said.

'No.'

He went and opened the back window. The air coming in only stirred up the smoke. Then he went and boldly opened the front door, and women shoppers had their first look at the mysterious gangland club. It showed nothing but age and a broken espresso machine. Still, the police and the federals had the phone tapped and almost every foot of the place bugged. You knew then that the secret life of the Mafia would soon exist only in court transcripts.

Now John Gotti is playing cards in his clubhouse, Bergin Hunt and Fish, on 101st Avenue. He concentrates on his hand. The priest from Nativity Church, just around the corner, comes in. Gotti pays rent for the outdoor carnival he is running in the church parking lot. The carnival consists of two games where children could win a teddy bear or a baseball cap. And ten different kinds of wheels, dice games and card games, all made legal by the seal of the Holy Roman Catholic Church. Walk on, policeman.

'Yeah?' Gotti says, not looking up at the priest.

'I've been watching the receipts for the last couple of nights,' the priest said. 'I think I should get twenty-five thousand dollars more.'

Gotti still does not look up from his cards. 'Sal, do you know how to give the last rites?'

'No, John.'

'Anthony, do you?'

'What is it, like extreme unction?' Anthony asks.

'Yeah.'

'I don't know nothin' like that.'

'We better get somebody,' Gotti says. 'Because when I look up from these here cards and I see a priest, I am goin' to kill the priest right here on the fuckin' floor, and I don't want to do that if we can't give him the last rites.'

Gotti put his cards down and looked up. The priest was gone.

Nobody could harm the Mafia on the magnitude of John Gotti's destructive flare-ups. He violated New York's revered rush-hour rules when he had Paul Castellano killed in the middle of it. It was brazen, and Gotti loved it. He had no idea of how this infuriated lawmen. As he never listened to anything but hosannas, he never heard the sound of tank treads on Mulberry Street. Right after they picked a jury for one big federal trial in Brooklyn, there was a line of cars in front of the Bergin Hunt and Fish club on 101st Avenue. Inside, they were plotting how to put all the people from the Gotti outfit, perhaps a thousand men, to work going door-to-door almost, to ask if somebody knew a juror. I watched the cars pull up and leave and was disturbed. Could these morons be capable of fixing a trial? Where was the FBI?

They found a street guy in the Astoria neighbourhood, Bosko Radonjich, who knew George Pape, who was a juror and was broke. Sammy Gravano bought him for sixty thousand dollars. During the trial, Andrew Maloney, the US Attorney, learned of the fix. He did not tell the prosecutor, Diane Giacalone, because he said catching everybody in the fix was more important. It was cheap and shameful.

Diane Giacalone was a soft flower and simultaneously a bundle of steel wiring. She came out of the neighbourhood, from the old Our Lady of Wisdom Academy a few doors up from 101st Avenue.

Always, she walked past the men who stood on the avenue as if they owned it. She knew who they were and thoroughly disliked them, Gotti foremost. Her father was an engineer who did not look to get rich. Hers was the great story, the finest example of fighting crime: a young woman raised amid mobsters who grew up to shatter them. The white males in dark suits in the US Attorney's office wanted her to drown. They had more than one of their tiny law-school classroom games going. They also had a stool pigeon in the Gotti line-up, a part Indian named Willie Boy Johnson.

So she had a fixed juror and a rat defendant, all unknown to her. The fixed jury acquitted. John Gotti ran out the back door of the courthouse and into a car that took him to a celebration at his Ravenite Club. He was the Teflon Don. You put me on trial, I fix your fucking jury and walk out in your face.

He was certain that it would remain like this forever. And during that party at the Ravenite, I was talking to Joe Butch, a tall, grey-haired guy who brought anisette and espresso to court. As we spoke, I noticed a door off in a corner. 'Where does that go?' I asked. Joe said it went upstairs. It sure did. Gotti used that door to go up to an apartment on the second floor where an old woman proudly let him hold his conferences. The apartment had more bugs than a flop house.

And there came a night in his clubhouse when Gotti, in overcoat and scarf, looked up to see uniformed cops walking in his clubhouse with FBI agents and federal warrants. He didn't argue. Whatever it was, he would beat it. In handcuffs, he walked out into the police car, and his last step on the sidewalk was the last of his life outside prison.

'We're the only fuckin' people in the whole courthouse that are any good,' he announced one day. 'The judge is no fucking good, the prosecutor is a motherfucking rat, and the girls he got working with him are fucking whores. The lawyers all should drown.'

Their eyes glistened with anticipation as the guards let them into the large, crowded courtroom where they could strut to the defence table with the entire throng watching every hair on Gotti's head, then shifting to his number two, Sammy 'the Bull' Gravano, who had a record of such violence that he, too, drew glances of excited awe.

That they could be going away for the rest of their lives only increased the drama. Gotti loved it. He knew that fear was a fraud, for he, John Gotti, could never be convicted anywhere on earth. Sammy didn't like it quite as much, but for now he would bask in the fame.

In court one day, they played a tape of Gotti's calling Gravano a stupid coward who shoots people in the back.

At day's end, as they were leaving the courtroom, Gravano put his face up to Gotti's and threatened him. Guards broke it up.

It took months, but before too long, Sammy Gravano, sitting in the misery of the Metropolitan Correctional Center in downtown Manhattan, told the guard that he wanted to see a federal agent. When the FBI heard that Gravano wanted to meet, they sent a platoon of agents to the jail. How would they like his testimony against John Gotti in exchange for his nineteen homicides? Wonderful, they said. They decided to get him out of there right away. The call was made to the control booth that Gravano was coming down. Guards and agents quietly brought him to the lobby. People in the control booth had the name Gotti up on the screen alongside Gravano's, because they regarded the two as the same, and if Gravano was being taken out, they figured, then so too was Gotti. So they brought him down also.

Gravano was in the lobby about to leave the building with the agents when the other elevator door opened and he saw Gotti inside.

'You're setting me up!' Gravano yelped at the agents.

One of them ran over to the elevator and told the guard to take Gotti back upstairs, where he went to bed in the first true pre-trial agony of his life, knowing what was coming.

Gravano walked out of the foul air of the Metropolitan Correctional Center and into the clear, chilly Manhattan night. Soon he would be called the most famous gang turncoat in the last half century.

On the witness stand, in a double-breasted suit and with quiet voice, Gravano put Gotti into murders. He described the Castellano shooting as if he was describing a schoolyard game. The mobsters met 'down water park', which is a playground in downtown Manhattan, along the East River. He went on and on without pause.

Soon the Ravenite clubhouse, a shabby cathedral of organised crime, was out of business. The former site was open for all on Mulberry Street to see. First it was a sumptuous dress shop, with an Asian woman standing in the middle of a row of expensive outfits. 'Gotti?' she said. 'I don't know who that is.'

Months later she was out of there, and in its place was a shoe store, which catered to feet made of gold.

Nor in Queens would you bother to walk down 101st Avenue. The kerb at the Bergin Hunt was empty. The clubhouse had been cut in half. A butcher was operating in a narrow shop, and he needed no card tables.

Meanwhile, Gotti is in my house. He is on a silver DVD that came in the mail from a guard at the Marion federal penitentiary, where the ex-gangster was in solitary several floors under the earth. I open the package, and here in my hands is over an hour of John Gotti talking about the Mafia, and I won't even transcribe it myself. I'll get somebody to do it. Because when you have a thing like this, clean work dropped in your lap, then it should be kept perfect. Before we know it this will be a book all its own, unsullied by my labour. Then I can pose and say how hard it was to get.

Good boy, Breslin.

And then my wife puts the DVD on and leaves the room as John Gotti appears on the screen. He is at a table in a cell with a phone in his hand. You see him through a window. Sitting there and listening is the back of some Ozone Park guy in a sweater. He holds a phone, too.

And John Gotti, the man who is going to make my life so much easier, starts off.

'You f——, c——, c———, f——.'

His right shoulder drops, and he sits there tilted.

'You f——n' hear me? You dopey f——n' c———. F——! S——— a——, p——— . . .'

He goes on and on and on and it covers more than one day, because suddenly his brother, Peter Gotti, is the visitor and then his daughter, Victoria, and even then Gotti doesn't change his tone or his language.

Here comes the reason the guard sent me the disc.

'Jimmy Breslin says I get mentioned fifty-one times in the papers. That's more than Abraham Lincoln.'

I listen through another twenty minutes of useless filthy language and then Gotti says: 'Nobody wants to f——n' help me, the dirty f——s. They don't f——n' do nothing. F—— them all. I go to Jimmy Breslin, and he puts me on the front page tomorrow. F—— all these f——s.'

He heaved as he spoke and tilted to his right some more, and I knew I wouldn't see him again, not strutting down Mulberry Street, or stepping into his car in Howard Beach with a guy holding the door for him, or signing autographs for women from out of town at Regine's nightclub on Madison Avenue, autographs and champagne for John Gotti, party of sixteen.

SEVENTEEN

Q: Mr Kaplan, can you tell the jury, who was Edward Lino?

A: Edward Lino was a captain in the Gambino crime family. Casso's relationship to Mr Lino wasn't very good. Casso thought that he was one of the people who tried to get him killed.

Q: Did Casso put out a contract on Edward Lino?

A: Yes. Probably originally around '87 or '88.

Q: Did Casso tell you the reasons, in addition to the attempted murder on him, the reasons that he wanted Edward Lino killed?

A: He said that he was one of the shooters in Paul Castellano's killing. Casso wanted to be – be involved in retribution for that, because it was unsanctioned.

Q: Did there come a time that Casso had a conversation with you regarding murdering Eddie Lino?

A: He wanted me to see if my two friends would take a contract on Eddie Lino. Louis Eppolito and Stephen Caracappa. I spoke to Louie and asked him if they wanted the contract.

Q: Did Casso specify a dollar amount?

A: Yes. sixty-five thousand dollars.

Q: When you offered the contract to Mr Eppolito, what did he say?

A: He said he would talk it over with Steve but that he couldn't see any reason for not taking it. He would get back to me in the next day.

Q: After Eppolito told you he was going to check with Steve, what happened next?

A: He came back and accepted the contract. Louie said that they would take the contract but they – they needed the car and they needed some guns. I went to see Anthony Casso and told him they needed guns.

Q: What happened?

A: Casso went into a big act, and he said, Don't these guys do anything for themselves? But he got – he got the two guns. I gave the guns to Louie Eppolito.

Q: Do you recall what types of guns at all?

A: One was an automatic and one was a revolver.

Q: How did you become familiar with guns?

A: I am not very familiar with guns, but I was in the navy. I fired some guns, and I know the difference between a revolver and an automatic. An automatic has a clip, and you put the clip into the gun, and it fires automatically. You can hold the trigger down, and it will keep firing. When you use a revolver, you put the bullets individually into a chamber around a circle, and it – pull the trigger one time for each shot.

Q: Did there come a time, Mr Kaplan, that you received eye surgery?

A: Yes. Three times.

Q: Did there come a time that you saw Mr Eppolito after having that surgery?

A: Yes. I was – it was about nine thirty or ten o'clock at night, and I was sleeping in the hospital. I had gotten my operation that day or the day before, and Louie came in the door, and he tapped me on the foot, and he woke me up, and first I jumped up when I seen him. I thought it was bad news. And I said, What's the matter? What's the matter? He said, No, no, take it easy. I got good news. I said, What? He says, We got Eddie Lino. I said, What do you mean you got him? He says, We killed him. And he went in his pocket, and he took out two newspaper articles about how a guy got pulled over on the Belt Parkway and got shot.

And I asked Louie how did he do it. He said, I followed him from the club on Avenue U, and he went on the Belt Parkway, and we turned on the light, and we pulled him over, and he pulled over on the grass, and I walked over to him and I said, Hey, Frankie, how are you? And Eddie got all happy. Then he says, I'm not Frankie Lino. I'm Eddie Lino. And Louie says, Oh, we thought you were Frankie Lino. And then Louie says, I pointed across to the passenger floor of the car and said, I asked Eddie Lino, What's that? And Eddie bent down to look, and Steve shot him a number of times.

Q: Mr Kaplan, did there come a time that you paid money for Eddie Lino's murder?

A: Yes. Anthony Casso sent it to my house.

Q: How much money did you pay?

A: When – it was a box full of money, a little box full of hundred-dollar bills. I counted it. There was seventy thousand dollars in it. I didn't know if Casso was testing me or what, because the agreed-upon price was sixty-five thousand dollars. I gave the money

to Louie, and I told him, I don't know if this
five thousand is for you or the guy is testing me.
If it's for you, keep it. If he's testing me, I'm going
to tell him about it and ask him if he wants
it back. And I said to Louie, Don't worry about it,
because we'll take the money off the next – next
month's four thousand.

Q: How did you get the money?

A: It was brought to me, and I had to – the big eye patch
on my head. A guy came to my door, rang the bell.
My wife answered the door, and he said he wanted to
see me. And my wife said, Why don't you come in?
He said, No, I don't want to come in. He stood at the
door, and he had a baseball cap over his head, and the
best of my ability I believe it was Georgie Zappola,
but I can't say for sure.

Q: Did Georgie – whoever that person was, whether it
was Georgie Zappola or whomever – did they hand
you that box?

A: He said, This is from Gas.

Q: How long after you got out of the hospital did the
person bring you the box of money?

A: Within two days.

Q: How long after getting the box of money did you give
it to Mr Eppolito?

A: The next day. I didn't want it. I wanted to pay the
bill.

Q: Did there ever come a time when you had a
conversation with Mr Eppolito about why Mr
Caracappa was the shooter?

A: In the hospital that night, I asked him how come if
he walked over to the car and had the conversation
with him, why did Steve shoot him? He said Steve
was the better shot.

In court, Burt Kaplan says to the prosecutor, 'I could use water.'

'Certainly.'

The prosecutor pours fresh cold water out of a decanter.

'Thank you very much.'

As he drinks, he stares at his former partners over the top of the glass.

Timmy Byrnes kept up with the trial testimony through newspapers and word of mouth. His honour was out there in everything Kaplan had to say.

Timmy is in the front room of the Byrnes Funeral Home in Gerritsen Beach, in Brooklyn, another of the low-sky neighbourhoods, where streets hold their feet into the first waters of the Atlantic.

The woman on the phone at the reception desk is saying, 'I'm so sorry for our loss, honey.'

In Gerritsen Beach even the funeral directors refer to the deceased as 'ours'.

In the chapel on this day is the late Elizabeth Ryan, age ninety-three. Timmy Byrnes is saying, 'If I wasn't running the funeral, I'd be going to it anyway.'

Timmy Byrnes is out of this neighbourhood and the family funeral parlour, and his is a way of life older than the street names. The corner outside is empty. All Brooklyn funeral homes have at least one saloon within eyeshot, but the Byrnes parlour seems to sit on a desert. This is only a disguise. Right across the street is a Veterans of Foreign Wars Post whose back door opens to the least push, especially that of a mourner. Inside, a great big bar serves all and at all hours.

It is a short distance, minutes, from Coney Island. A parkway runs alongside wetlands and water, with inlets streaming under bridges to clusters of houses. Gerritsen Beach has streets of two-storey brick houses made graceful by sturdy maple trees. Then the brick homes end at alleys of wood houses, many in a jumble at a narrow slip of water filled with small, odd boats. The water widens and, sparkling, runs out to a bay and the pounding ocean just beyond.

It isn't big-city life. It doesn't have easy mass transit. The B31 bus is a sixteen-minute ride to the Kings Highway subway stop of the Q train. Then it is half an hour more to Manhattan. At the start of the line, the B31 stops in front of Resurrection Roman Catholic Church and school, dull red-stone buildings that cover a block and are large and ominous enough to look like a Catholic Pentagon.

Of course it isn't Tribeca or Lincoln Center or any of the other districts within a walk or a quick subway ride of the jobs of such great importance, such as investment banker, corporate lawyer. It is one of the few neighbourhoods of the city where police officers live.

Timmy Byrnes is Catholic, Irish, marines, bachelor's degree, master's degree, police department, detective, lieutenant, captain. Retired as an inspector. Funeral director. At all times the passion is to protect and serve. He is sixty-two now and looks forty-five. He is strikingly handsome, thin, with tousled light hair, blue eyes that are warm and notice everything, and a good smile.

Long ago, Timmy Byrnes worked with Louis Eppolito in the Senior Citizens Robbery Unit, Brooklyn South. Timmy had worn shield number 3179, one of the famous gold-and-blue detective shields of the New York Police Department. Timmy put it up there on the dresser when he went to sleep. The badge, his monument, his statue, was the outward personification of everything he was.

Who knew that someday Louie Eppolito would get Timmy Byrnes's badge number 3179 and betray everyone who ever wore it, betray all honour, betray an entire way of life that was the sinew of Brooklyn and the heart of its honesty?

This, rather than Mrs Ryan, for whom I would offer a prayer anyway, is what brings me to the old funeral home.

Louie Eppolito was promoted to detective on 1 July 1977. As with everything else to do with him, there was the hint of lousiness. Tim Byrnes remembers, 'What I was told was that he had an order from the chief of personnel saying he was to be made a detective, and the personnel guy retired, and Louie busted in on the new chief of detectives and showed him the letter, and the chief said, "Well, you're a detective." I don't know if the letter was real or not. But Louie carried it off.'

New York City has a most sophisticated screening for police candidates, yet Caracappa, with a burglary conviction – and not as a kid breaking into a gas station but as a member of a professional burglary ring – passed all screening. On 5 January 1960, at the age of seventeen, he was arrested for grand larceny on Staten Island. He and an accomplice rented a truck – it was needed because they were not stealing by the handful – and ransacked a lumberyard for building materials for which they had a buyer. Caracappa was given youthful-offender status for a felony. The records were sealed. There was no sentence. Maybe there should have been.

Certainly the police department had no right to allow him to go out into the public with a badge and gun. They turn applicants down because of traffic violations and street quarrels. Caracappa should not have been allowed to take the test. That he did take it, that he passed and became a patrolman and then that he was made a detective and up the grades, that he did all this with a background that said to anybody, I am a criminal and I might even shoot for money, just about screams 'fix' or 'fixes' or 'continuing fix'.

Can you tell me how Louis Eppolito became a cop? He came from a Mafia family. His father killed people. His uncle was known as Jimmy the Clam, and he lived as a mobster and died as a mobster. The son, Louie's cousin, was murdered by the mob.

Tim Byrnes became a detective because of his hard work and because everyone trusted him. He took shield 3179. Sometimes he looked at the badge for long moments. Lord, what a beautiful thing. Put that shield out on the dresser and stare at it for as many minutes as you have.

Tim Byrnes worked the streets and put up so much of his life to study for promotion exams. He became a sergeant in 1974 and was named squad commander for the Sixtieth Precinct, on West Eighth and Surf Avenue in Coney Island. His badge changed with the title.

He turned in 3179 at the Shield Desk in police headquarters and was given a sergeant's badge.

If Byrnes had had a brother, a son, or a cop he worked with, he could have had 3179 reserved for them. He had nobody. Or if this had been some cheap jersey for a sports team, Timmy's number would have been retired with tears and tumult. But he only carried that number when he was out trying to save lives, to protect people. He did it day or night, did it with a tonne of bravery and a cop's common sense.

Lou Eppolito came to work with that same badge and his jacket over his shoulder, his collar open, his black hair full, his voice bawling. Big-city detective. He is supposed to carry a Smith & Wesson .38 with a four-inch barrel. His off-duty is supposed to be a Colt with a two-inch barrel. He came roaring into the precinct with a six-inch Ruger. Who said he could do this? I got permission from Sullivan. This was the chief of detectives. Byrnes spoke to Sullivan, who thought he might have spoken to Eppolito but he wasn't sure, and besides, isn't it late to bother with it? Eppolito had bulled his way through again.

Every time Byrnes saw Eppolito, he noticed that shield hanging from his breast pocket or on the chain around his neck. Three one seven nine.

The senior citizens squad of Brooklyn South was set up to try to protect the elderly in the area, mostly Jewish, from attacks by the waves of the young, who were of colour. Daily life can hardly get any uglier.

The big street, Flatbush Avenue, was one small store after another, block after block of them, with some larger chain outlets breaking up the alignment. Some of the blocks had three and four furniture stores, whose signs proclaimed full bedroom sets for affordable money.

The homes were apartment houses or two-storey unattached frames. From these streets came old women out food shopping and then home to apartments where an ageing husband waited or, more often, to the emptiness left by widowhood and children off and married. For Louie Eppolito it was a million-dollar assignment. He could wrap his arms around an old Jewish woman out of a concentration camp and soothe her. Don't worry, Mama. I'm here.

Byrnes was called one night to an apartment where one of the young had pushed in after an old woman and was robbing her when Louie Eppolito, running a raiding party, arrived. Louie beat the kid senseless. The blood was over the room like fresh paint.

'You told him,' Byrnes said. 'I don't think it did any good.'

Soon Eppolito decides he is detective of the century, pounding down Flatbush Avenue. He sounds like an ice-cream truck. Chiming in the air are the gold shield and all his medals on a chain around his neck. In his wallet, he had a picture of an ape with a criminal-identification licence plate around his neck. Louie would say, 'Here is my Most Wanted.'

Does he have medals? He is the eleventh-most-decorated cop in the city. Yes, he is. He reports this to you himself. That is what he will swear to. Detective Eppolito of the senior citizens squad, protector of the aged, pounding after this kid who has just stolen an old lady's purse.

Louie's big paws clout the kid on the shoulders and drive him into the sidewalk.

'They come in here on the Soul Train, and they think they can rob our decent seniors,' Louie exults.

The kid is booked. And Louie Eppolito is right back on Flatbush Avenue. He bursts into the storefront office of the *Courier-Life*, which publishes weekly papers that cover the area.

'I just collared a kid was about to murder a senior on Glenwood Road. He had a .38 in his pocket. He was going to use it on her. Then maybe turn it on me. But he got a look at me and he took off. I got him all right. Don't fuckin' worry about Louie's running,' he assured the reporters. 'You fellas ought to be onto what we're doing. I made more collars than anybody in Brooklyn this week. Twenty-five arrests! Where is the photographer? People see my picture, they fuckin' well know.'

In handling domestic-violence calls, he first got the husband outside and beat him blind. Then he went back later to see the wife. 'Battered wives were the most vulnerable,' he said. 'Every time we went on a call where a husband smacked his wife, I went back that night and smacked it to her, too.'

Now Eppolito is retired in Las Vegas. There, he and a guy from Jamaica, Queens, Jackie Rosaludi, earning a good living as a stunt man and actor, are reminiscing.

'Khe Sanh,' Louie says. 'That was hell.'

'You were there?' Jackie says.

'Oh, yeah. Marines.'

'I was in the marines,' Jackie says. 'Two oh oh one seven seven eight.'

That was the military serial number and it becomes part of your name. Nobody forgets it.

'What's yours?' he asks Louie.

'Gee, I can't remember it right now,' Louie says.

He was never in, Jackie says to himself. He listens in wonderment at the ease and extent of this guy's lying.

'Ever since Khe Sanh, I been ready,' Louie says. He shows a .38 inside his belt. And a derringer.

'What do you need the derringer for?' Jackie asks.

'You never know,' Louie says. 'We never knew at Khe Sanh.'

The day Jackie decided that some disturbing darkness was moving underneath Louie's big, loud front came when he was out with Louie and Louie's son in Las Vegas and they stopped at a baseball-card shop. Jackie, a collector, bought a hundred dollars' worth of cards. Back in the car, Louie showed his son three hundred cards that he had lifted from the store.

'Another hour and I could've had the whole store,' he told the kid proudly.

Then there was a night in Manhattan, when Jackie wanted to stop at a pizza place and Louie insisted they go instead to some restaurant. He remembers how Louie proudly described his background, his

Mafia lineage. 'I'm Fat's son,' he boasted. 'Fat was a Mafia hit man. I'm Jimmy's nephew.'

Louie spent the entire hour and a half during dinner looking to his left, at the restaurant door.

'He'll be here,' Louie said.

'Who?' Jackie said.

'Gotti. This is his place.'

He didn't show.

There came a night when Louie's grandmother was in the Torregrossa Funeral Home on Avenue U, and Louie, coming from work, was in jeans and a leather jacket. When they reached the funeral parlour, he told Jackie that he would sit in the car. He wasn't dressed for a wake. He said he would try tomorrow. It didn't matter. 'She is just like a dead cat in the street.'

Swaggering and swinging, Louie Eppolito had heard other cops talking about Dan O'Leary of the Seventy-first Precinct, who was a boxing instructor and could fight more than somewhat. Eppolito didn't have to hear it a lot. There was going to be a smoker in Izzy Zwerling's Gym, two flights up from Church Avenue, only steps away from Erasmus Hall High School, where Louie had won the first award of his life, for body-building. Now he wanted to box Dan O'Leary in the smoker. When the other cops heard of the proposal, Eppolito versus O'Leary, heavyweights, they were immediately excited and began betting. Irish versus Italian. Eppolito said he couldn't wait for the match to prove to the entire police department that he was the champion of all who wore blue.

Dan O'Leary thought, Why does he want to fight me so much? Then he shrugged. Another fight.

He received in the mail an unsigned condolence card. It was not a good idea. Who else would have sent him that taunt?

I had an idea of what O'Leary was like. I talked to Denis Hamill of the *Daily News*, and he told me about O'Leary and Eppolito and gave me O'Leary's phone number. 'Tell him I told you to call. Even better, tell him Pudgy Walsh told you.' Pudgy Walsh is the coach of a Brooklyn sandlot football team that is known all over the country. O'Leary used to play. So I called O'Leary and got a tape and announced that Pudgy Walsh had told me to call. I left a number but never heard back.

Later I asked Bob Nardoza of the US Attorney's office if he could put me in touch with O'Leary. Nardoza is one of the most efficient communications people I've ever known. A day later, I got a call.

'This is Dan O'Leary. You called me, and I never returned your call. You said that Pudgy Walsh told you to call. Well, I called Pudgy Walsh, and he said he never spoke to you. That's why I didn't call you back. You told a lie.'

'All right,' I said. 'I guess that rules me out with you.'

'No, it doesn't. It means that you shouldn't lie to me. You never should have said that you talked to Pudgy Walsh about me when you never did.'

He was Irish. He also would have enjoyed the Third Punic War. He is 6 ft 2 in. and weighed 240 on this night. He had that straight face that demands it his way, tell me the truth, and a pair of very good-size hands.

Eppolito was so pleased with himself that he could not envision anything getting in his way. Notably not Dan O'Leary. In a crowded third-floor gym, Louie Eppolito came out of his corner like a steer out of a rodeo chute, snorting, filled with rage, and he threw a roundhouse left hook that was meant to kill.

Weight lifters who try boxing have some difficulty in addressing an opponent, in that their arms have trouble reaching the front of their body. Eppolito's left hook was a full six inches out there in the smoky air.

O'Leary picked it off with his glove. A bee.

Eppolito threw a second left hook that was more vicious than the first.

O'Leary's glove picked this one off, too. Another bee. I thought I chased you before.

O'Leary threw a straight hand into Eppolito's face. Now he

jabbed. Jabbed once, then he doubled up. And so it went. 'I was triple-jabbing him,' O'Leary remembers.

The fight was scheduled for three two-minute rounds.

Somewhere in the second round, Eppolito was trying to swallow all the air in the room. He could not get enough. Soon, jabs and straight rights had him on crazy street.

They stopped the fight. Somebody who had an idea of what the match might become had brought oxygen to the gym. Eppolito needed it. There goes the toughness that arrives on a loud voice.

This is 6 November 1990. Timmy Byrnes is on patrol when there comes a call about a car with a dead man on the grass alongside the Belt Parkway, where it runs in front of Gerritsen Beach. He answers the call and sees a car with the front door open. The body inside is slumped with the head almost to the floor. The guy had been shot in the back of the skull.

The supervisors coming on the scene are talking about a possible roadside mugging gone bad. Byrnes considers the car, on the grass with the door open. Nobody pulls to the side of the road like that unless it is for somebody he knows well, or for police, Byrnes tells himself. He tells an inspector in charge, 'This is OC.' Organised crime.

He also knows immediately that when they lay this body out, they are going to have to put the head on the right-hand side as you approach the coffin, instead of the standard left, for the bullet had gone in with a neat hole but had caused an ugly exit wound.

This had him wondering about the shooting for a long time. Timmy Byrnes heard other detectives complaining that the FBI knew something about it and would not tell. The victim was Eddie Lino. Byrnes didn't know much about Lino except that he was a gangster with the Gambinos of John Gotti. But now he heard whispers, cops coming in off the streets and talking in toilets, and it all told him to picture his shield, 3179. Picture Louie Eppolito pulling Eddie Lino over on the parkway. The gold badge flashes in the gunfire that murdered Eddie Lino.

Now in the family funeral home in Gerritsen Beach, he reads what I have brought along: Burt Kaplan's sworn account of how Louie Eppolito disgraced the badge that Timmy had worn so proudly.

Timmy flinches.

EIGHTEEN

Q: Mr Kaplan, did Anthony Casso ever put out a murder
contract on you?

A: Yes.

This development came in the early '90s, after Burt Kaplan
got a phone call one night from Lou Eppolito. He said that a
massive sweep was going to be made next morning of suspects
in the mob's scheme to profit from the New York City Housing
Authority's window-replacement project. The term 'replacement
windows' sounds unpromising, but the mobsters knew better. They
were stealing two dollars per replacement window and the city was
buying almost a million of them. Kaplan called Casso, who wasn't
home. He then called Casso's co-boss Vic Amuso. 'I'll come around
in the morning,' Amuso said. Kaplan said no, get over here now.
Amuso came in a hurry. He listened to what Kaplan had to say.

'I'll go home and pack,' Amuso said.

'I would leave right now,' Kaplan said. 'I wouldn't go home.'

Amuso was gone by late night. Casso got word and also
immediately disappeared. He was not seen for the next three years.
Amuso went to Johnstown, Pennsylvania, and lasted a short time
before he began telephoning most of Brooklyn. He found a pizzeria
where he could hang out. But he was so used to being a man of
honour and importance that he had to tell the waitress, 'What do I

do? Me, I'm a gangster.' Soon the waitress was replaced by a team of six FBI agents, and he never saw the outside again.

Gaspipe found a house in the woods at Budd Lake in New Jersey, which he decorated expensively, including with a woman.

Q: When was that?

A: I believe it was 1993. I was harbouring, helping
           harbour Anthony Casso when he was on the lam from
           the government. I used to meet him, I used to take
           his wife to him, and the last time I had – was taking
           his wife to him, we stopped at a hotel because I had
           to go to the bathroom. It was a hotel that I normally
           got rooms in for Casso and his wife under my name,
           and I was going to meet him someplace else this
           particular day, but this hotel was on the way, and I
           had to use the men's room, and I asked her, I said, I'd
           like to stop at that hotel because I have to go to the
           bathroom. And we stopped there, and we got – I got
           out of the car. She stood in the car, and I seen two
           gentlemen in a car who to me definitely resembled
           FBI agents, you know, the typical sunglasses and the
           unmarked car with the antennas, and I looked at them,
           and I went in and used the bathroom, and when I
           came out, I said to her, to Lillian Casso, I said, I think
           there's FBI agents in the parking lot. And I drove by
           them and let her see them, and then I said, I think
           we should drive around for a half an hour or so before
           we meet Anthony and see if I could spot anybody tailing
           me. And I took her to a parking lot in a shopping mall,
           and I let her out, and I told her tell her husband what
           I said about seeing the people, and I would drive away,
           and he would come and meet her or send somebody to
           meet her and take her to where he was.

When I saw him Monday, when I picked up his wife to take her home – this originally started on a Saturday – and I met him in the parking lot of the same shopping mall, and I said, Anthony, I think you should be careful because it looks like to me there was definitely agents there, and the hotel room was under my name, and I think he should be very careful.

And the next day he got arrested, and the fact that I warned him, he put it in his head that I was the one who gave him up, and unbeknownst to me he put a contract out on me, which I didn't find out about until I was arrested in '96. When I went to MDC and I was locked up, three or four people told me they had pleaded to the conspiracy to kill me for Anthony Casso.

Q: When was the last – sorry, Mr Kaplan, you were going to say something else?

THE COURT: Strike that last testimony about what he was told.

Q: You said you learned about a murder contract against you.

A: Yes.

Q: Who did you speak to about that?

A: George Zappola, Frank Papagni, Michael Bloom.

Q: Did you have a relationship with them at the time that they had that conversation with you?

A: Yes. I was friends with them.

The arrest of Gaspipe came about not because of anything Kaplan said or did but because Casso, like Vic Amuso, had an overpowering need to talk. He had made call after call from Budd

Lake to the phone of Frank Lastorino, a fellow hoodlum. Casso phoned Lastorino at night. He phoned early in the morning. He phoned after his Jersey girlfriend left for work. A little detective work followed. One day, Casso failed to make his usual call when he came out of the shower, because his hands were in cuffs. He was hauled off to a detention cell in New York, where he faced about fifty major charges. He pled guilty and said he would be a witness against two cops who were doing murders for him. He would testify against Burt Kaplan and anybody else the government wanted, too.

> **Q:** After Casso's arrest, did there come a time that he asked you for information regarding a federal prosecutor and a federal judge?
>
> **A:** Yes. The judge was Judge Nickerson, and the prosecutor was Charlie Rose.
>
> **Q:** What did Casso ask you to do?
>
> **A:** Get their addresses, where they lived.
>
> **Q:** Did you bring that request to Mr Eppolito or Mr Caracappa?
>
> **A:** Yes.
>
> **Q:** Did they refuse to do that?
>
> **A:** Absolutely refused.
>
> **Q:** Did they give a reason for that?
>
> **A:** They didn't want to get involved. It would bring too much heat.

As you can imagine, the attempt by Casso to murder Burt Kaplan put some strain on their friendship.

> **Q:** Tell the jury, sir, did Mr Casso live in a house you owned?

A: Yes. Casso came to me and – in, I believe it was 1985, and he said that he wanted to move into a bigger house and that he wanted me to buy his house. I said, Anthony, I really don't want your house, and I'm happy where I'm at. He says, Yeah, but I trust you, and I'm going to sell you the house cheap, and you can make a profit on it, and I really don't want the whole world to know that I'm selling my house, and I need the money so that I can show it when I buy the bigger house. He was buying Fortunoff's house. Fortunoff's, the department store.

Q: So Mr Casso moved into a house you owned?

A: No, he owned the house originally, and he stayed in the house while he was building the house on Fortunoff's property.

Q: Did he ever live in a house you owned?

A: That's the same house. He lived with his wife, his son and his daughter.

Q: And is anybody from his family still in that house?

A: His son.

Q: What happened to Mrs Casso?

A: She died recently from a stroke.

Q: Did you have any communications with Mrs Casso since 1993?

A: Yes. Once. She asked my wife if she could visit me in Allenwood, if I would put her on my visiting list, because she wanted to speak to me about buying the house back.

Q: What were the terms of her purchase of the house as Mrs Casso proposed them to you?

A: Originally she said she would give me back my

money, and I also told her that her son-in-law owed me some money that he didn't pay me, and I wanted the purchase plus the interest I paid on the mortgage, and the money the son-in-law owed me, and she said OK, and then she changed her mind and said, I want the house for nothing.

Q: What happened?

A: I wouldn't give it to her. Why would I give it to her?

Q: Today do you still own that house?

A: Yes. I just served her son with an eviction notice through a lawyer.

NINETEEN

On a day in June 2005, Sammy the Bull Gravano is in the town of Hackensack, New Jersey, the county seat of Bergen County. It is just across the George Washington Bridge from Manhattan. Looking out the window in Hackensack, you can see the skyline. It is a thousand miles away.

All the cement in between seemed to speak for all the bodies left under roadways by Gravano, who was in handcuffs while being lugged out of a van in the empty parking lot and into a suburban courthouse where homicide cases usually arrive under the headine WIFE KNIFES HUSBAND.

Gravano was in the painful silence of the end of informing. He was also sick with this Graves' disease, which has to do with the thyroid. It had pulled out his hair and left a head that was bald and pink. Folds of flesh were in place of eyebrows.

Once, years before, Lou Eppolito and Steve Caracappa had supposedly tried but been unable to blow Sammy away, according to Burt Kaplan. Who can remember why? All these men had ample reasons for wanting one another deceased.

The killer cops staked out Gravano's construction company on Stillwell Avenue in Brooklyn. They followed Gravano to his house a few times. They also staked out Tali's bar and grill on Eighteenth Avenue, where Gravano hung out. But Sammy continued to live.

Q: What did Santora tell you had happened?

A: He told me that they stopped surveilling the business,
           because a detective who knew Louie or Steve came
           up to them in a car and started a conversation with
           them about how you doing, what are you doing here,
           and they said they are just there to meet somebody,
           and they didn't think they should go to that spot
           any more. They followed Gravano to his house and
           from his house on a lot of occasions, but they could
           never catch him alone. They told me he was too
           cautious and [was] always dropped off by somebody.

Maybe Gravano would have been better off if the cops had
completed that particular piece of work. He lived to sit here in near
anonymity in a small-town courtroom in New Jersey where nobody
cared enough to come look at him.

'I want to take a polygraph,' he said. 'I want the others to take a
polygraph, too.'

'We can't force people in this state to take polygraphs,' the judge
said.

Gravano wanted something like that because there was no way he
was guilty of this particular homicide.

Once Gravano was known as 'the Bull', and when he came to a
major federal courthouse in Brooklyn, he arrived by helicopter with
television cameras catching him from a distance, with FBI agents
walking ahead and alongside with their trouser cuffs flapping in the
harbour wind. The sidewalks in front of the courthouse were always
filled with cameramen.

There was, on this Jersey morning, no television truck nor caravan
of unmarked police cars. Only a state trooper dressed like General
Patton standing at the entrance to the courthouse parking lot.

'Keep going, keep going.'

He waves away the morning air. Behind him, Gravano was
being unloaded. Some yards down, at the courthouse ground-floor
entrance, another guard, a little man, is standing at the door with

his hands out. 'No, not open,' he says. There were maybe ten people waiting. Then came a rasp over a hand radio. Gravano was inside safely and the guard was gone. People walked in. The guard was running a metal detector. After his machine was another metal detector. Up one flight to the courtroom floor, where there was another.

The halls were lined with Bergen County sheriffs in the running for the avoirdupois championship of East Coast law enforcement.

Inside the courtroom I took a seat in the empty first row. The doorway on the side of the courtroom was open to a corridor crowded with lawmen the size of living-room couches. There were only a few people in the pews and not one news reporter until a man with a pad and pen slid in alongside us. He was Kibret Markos from the *Bergen Record*.

'I didn't know this was going on,' he said. 'I was walking past the building, and I saw the new metal detector, and I decided to see what was up.'

The prosecutor, Wayne Mello, thin, tanned, in a dark suit and salmon tie, came over to say hello to Jerry Capeci, whose Gang Land site on the Internet is quite famous. Mello had the dress and manner of a politician prowling for more career. He was, however, in an empty courtroom out of which could only come the enemy of ambitions, apathy.

He had the only murder case that could be called silly. Twenty-five years ago, Richard 'Iceman' Kuklinski was arrested for killing a New York detective, Peter Calabro, in a gangland-style hit on a Saddle River, New Jersey, road. All these years later and Kuklinski had a jailhouse interview on television and announced he had killed the cop. 'I should know. I killed more than a hundred people,' he announced. 'I killed him for Sammy Gravano,' he announced. 'Sammy don't like cops.'

This allowed him to be featured in three HBO specials. And had Gravano indicted for killing a cop here in Bergen County, where he never was.

'I never heard of the fucking guy,' Gravano said. 'Why would I get some guy hit over here when he was a cop down in New York all the time whenever I wanted him, which I didn't.'

Gravano, for a time America's greatest stool pigeon, was listed as being in prison somewhere. Maybe in Florence, Colorado, where they keep human beings thirty-one feet underground and are proud of it, or in Phoenix, Arizona, where the sheriff has convicts sleep in tents in the hundred-degree heat. Wherever you looked or called, they said Gravano was not there. He was hidden, like an heirloom, in the Witness Protection Program.

Kuklinski, in Trenton State Prison, sat down with Gravano's lawyer, Anthony Ricco. He took a legal pad and wrote in pencil in a heavy hand that he would 'make the case go away' and clear Gravano for two hundred thousand.

He showed this to Gravano's lawyer and his associate.

He then tore the page into small pieces and put them into his mouth and, like an old bookmaker with bet slips, swallowed hard.

'Now yez know what I want, but you can't show nobody proof against me for extortion,' he said. 'This is how a real criminal does it. And I'm a real criminal.'

Ricco looked at the yellow pad. The indent left by Kuklinski's heavy hand on the next page was completely readable. A laboratory could raise it in letters as large as those on a billboard. The next day Gravano's lawyer, Ricco, asked that the murder charge against Gravano be thrown out. The judge is holding a hearing on the matter.

A sheriff came to the front of the room to announce, 'The judge does not like gum chewing in the room. He'll call you on it.'

The only people who appeared to be chewing gum were about half the sheriffs.

Looking through the pack of sheriffs in the doorway, you got a glimpse of a pale blue prison shirt. Suddenly, without a rustle, Gravano, in handcuffs, came through the door.

Long ago, Sammy 'the Bull' Gravano was out on bail for one trial, and in the mornings before court he came down the hill to Gleason's, a fight gym at the end of the street leading from the court to the East

River. Sammy sparred with Eduardo Viruet, a trainer. More than a trainer. Viruet had boxed twice, going the distance each time, against Roberto Duran, who around then was maybe the best fighter in the universe. To start his gym workout, Gravano rushed at Viruet. He threw a punch. 'Oooohhhh!' Viruet said. He had picked the punch off with his elbow. 'You're so strong today. You will hurt me.' Gravano threw a punch at Eduardo's jaw. 'Ooooohhhh!' Viruet said. The punch grazed a moving chin, if it even did that. Gravano went three rounds, during which he was sure he was crippling Viruet. He has not hit Viruet yet. Nor has Viruet hit Gravano. The urge to throw twenty-five punches into Gravano's face was almost overwhelming. Viruet's pocket prevailed. You do not punch the rent.

Gravano paid Viruet three hundred dollars for the rounds and paid it every day. Gravano swaggered out with a big guy who drove him.

'The big guy is not the big guy,' Viruet told trainer Teddy Atlas. 'The little guy is the big guy.'

Gravano was allowed to drop his nineteen murders into the courtroom trash basket and go off into the Arizona sunset. He suddenly had a life again. But a man living with crime in his blood knows only villainy. Gravano tried to corner the Ecstasy trade. It is a pill that causes instant chaos. He threatened dealers with the same frightful carnage as he caused in Brooklyn. His reputation was his weapon. He brought his wife, son and daughter into the business with him. The four were arrested. He had shucked off nineteen murders and was back in a prison jumpsuit.

The Ecstasy case went into Brooklyn. Sammy was brought back to the federal courthouse, on Cadman Plaza. He sat with defendants who were in their twenties, a couple of them, poor fools, in college. Disease had sucked the weight and muscle off Sammy and put a gallon of fright into his blood. He could not control his shaking. He kept looking behind him at the spectators as if they were Gotti murderers who would rush up and strangle him. He was shipped back to prison in Arizona for more courtroom, which is his life at the end of so much murder and informing.

TWENTY

Liz Hydell, Jimmy's sister, found out during the trial that Caracappa was living under house arrest in his mother's place on Kramer Street in Staten Island, around the corner from her own mother's house on Grasmere Avenue. Elizabeth Hydell drove around the corner and got out at Caracappa's house. 'I was scared to death, but I was going to do it,' she said. She went up the front walk and rang the bell. She heard a noise, and Caracappa came out of the alley from behind the house.

'Who are you looking for?' she remembers him asking.

'You.'

'Who are you?' he asked.

'Jimmy Hydell's sister. You motherfucker. I want to see you when they put handcuffs on you and take you away for the rest of your life.'

She remembers Caracappa saying something about calling his lawyer, and then he went back up the alley.

'I'll see you,' she called.

Staten Island is a large landmass that steps out of the harbour of the city with its two wide, deep channels – the Buttermilk and the Narrows – both able to handle aircraft carriers, supertankers and common traffic of ferry-boats and weekend sail-boats. A slender stretch of water on the far side of the island separates it from New Jersey.

Freighters and great liners move through the sparkling water and pass under the Verrazano Bridge into the harbour or into the first rolling waters of the Atlantic. Always, tugboats throw white water into the sky.

The island became the protectorate for the Mafia beginning in the late 1950s. Steadily, as people of colour spread through Brooklyn, the city realigned itself. The Italians left East New York and Canarsie and Bensonhurst for Staten Island. Of the tens and tens of thousands of Italians who crossed the bridge, there were a few who owned police records attesting to their membership in the Mafia.

Staten Island changed Mafia life, which went from walk-ups with fire escapes running down the fronts, from streets of pork stores and funeral parlours, from clubhouses and small restaurants with cars pulling into kerbs for conferences, into neighbourhoods of semi-suburban streets with imitation mansions.

While he lived, the boss of the Mafia, Paul Castellano, did so in a large white house with a circular driveway in an area of Staten Island called Todt Hill. So many other mobsters try even now to imitate him. They want big, which is easier to have on Staten Island than in the other boroughs, and isolation. You leave the wife in the large gleaming kitchen and the kids in school, and they are all safe while you roam through the rest of the city and have fun with your girlfriends.

Hylan Boulevard, the road going along the south shore of the island, the ocean side, is a parking lot. The stores are Nails, Hair, a Subaru car lot lined with flags, Goodfellas, Bueno Jewelers, Agua 'newly decorated banquet room', A Class Limousine, Tattoo, Wok, Nails, 122nd Precinct, Excelsior Grand Catering Hall. You go off into these Mafia cul-de-sacs, one of which, Nicolosi Loop, has big mansions with gargoyles and stone lions in front. Number 57, the FBI sheet informs, is the home of Richard Cantarella, true mobster. A house on another block has an elevator visible through the large window running from just over the front door to the peak of the roof. This has to be the home of an absolute mass murderer.

Gaspipe Casso had eight pay phones around Staten Island that he used to talk to Eppolito and Caracappa when he was on the lam.

Remain driving and you are on Barlow Avenue, where Anthony Rotondo lived in a brick ranch house that is larger by far than the regular one-family frames owned by legitimate people. He sold drugs and was involved with murders and then became a stool pigeon and got lost in witness protection. Somebody currently lives in the house but answers no doorbells or knocks.

The children rarely go to public schools. They can be found in St Joseph Hill Academy, which is near Paul Castellano's old house on Todt Hill. The wives and other family women drive to the expensive Short Hills shopping centre in New Jersey. 'No Brooklyn Eighty-sixth Street,' one woman answered when asked where she shopped.

Federal raids keep snatching twenty and thirty at a time. Many collapse during the ride to the FBI offices and give up everybody they know and their brothers, too, if needed. They crowd into the Witness Protection Program and leave Staten Island for good. The stand-up guys say nothing and pronounce their names clearly to an intake officer at a federal penitentiary, also far away.

In legitimate life, Staten Island votes race and Italian Republican. The revered politician is Rudolph Giuliani, who filled the jails as a federal prosecutor in New York. You have Staten Island people shivering with excitement at a prosecutor becoming a president but simultaneously approving of these big tough mafiosos.

People outside Staten Island like to talk about the end of organised crime, but here they know there will always be a Mafia. Just like during Prohibition, mobsters will do things nobody else wants to do. They will find little services that nobody else will provide. There is shortly going to be a great big Indian casino in a desolate part of New York called Monticello. As soon as it opens, they will have to find somebody to supply clean tablecloths and napkins and sheets and towels. They will need somebody else to haul away garbage. Somebody else will have to park the cars. And for the gamblers, private banking will be needed. Somebody will have to lend them money once even the credit-card companies turn them away. The Mafia will offer all this and more.

Here in the dawn was Sal Reale's Mercedes, its exhaust a white spiral in the dark sky and snow on Sutter Avenue in Ozone Park, Queens. He was known as John Gotti's man at Kennedy Airport, to which he could almost walk. He was head of Local 851 of the Teamsters, which meant he was in charge of the snowploughs that clear the runways and ramps to let big jets tear into the sky.

The airlines will pay anything to have the runways cleared so their planes can take off. If they do not pay, the Teamsters' drivers in Reale's union will not plough. It is that simple. Either you see your planes taking off on a cleared runway or you stare out the window at them sitting in deep snow.

At this same dawn hour, in Woodmere, Long Island, the shortest of drives to the airport, Harry Davidoff runs out of his house like a child going sledding. He whoops it up in the falling snow.

Harry was the president of Teamsters Local 295, which is alongside Sal Reale in their union headquarters at the airport.

Harry Davidoff was one of the Davidoff brothers of Brownsville, in Brooklyn. Harry is known as 'Little Gangy', and he has a brother, 'Big Gangy', who at this time was well away in a state prison, and Avrom or 'Boomy' or 'Bummy', last name changed to Davis for fight show cards. He was considered the non-violent man of the family. In a main event at Madison Square Garden, he got mad and fouled the other fighter ten straight times before the cops reached the ring. He died chasing a couple of hold-up men out of a saloon he had just sold to a friend. Everybody loved him, and he had the biggest funeral Brownsville ever saw.

Reale and Big Gangy got to the union offices early to take the first frantic calls from airlines.

Once they had Delta for $300,000 a year, whether eight feet of snow fell or no snow at all. The money ensured that the airline would be the first to have ramps and runways cleared and planes in the sky.

There were other paid-up airlines being serviced right at this moment. A hundred thousand from this one, another hundred thousand from the next. A good snowfall was worth two million, Sal Reale said. 'That's for one snow. The next snow is another two million or so.'

The paws of the mob did not stop there. Snow had to be carted away from the airport. It was taken by truck to the Canarsie landfill, which was only a short drive away. Each truckload cost a coupon that went for a hundred and fifty dollars and was paid by the union. They bought thousand-dollar books of coupons. A man sat at the landfill entrance in a wood shack with a pot-bellied stove and a small window from which he directed many trucks to enter on the exit side, which had no electronic device counting the number of trucks passing through. Only the trucks he directed to the entrance lane paid the coupon. The others gave him fifty dollars instead of the coupon. The city lost millions that way. The mobsters tried every way there was to cheat. If there was no snow, then you could always steal rolls of butterscotch candies from airport news-stands.

'Harry Davidoff had so much money piled in his house he couldn't see his wife,' Reale said.

TWENTY-ONE

Q: Did your family have any sway over you in terms of your decision to cooperate?

A: Yes and no. My wife and my daughter been asking me to cooperate from the first day, and I didn't do it. And my daughter adopted a grandchild from Russia, and he's two and a half years old now. I wanted someday to be able to spend some time with him. But I can't honestly say I did this for my family. I did it, in all honesty, because I felt that I was gonna be made the scapegoat in this case.

Q: You said your family asked you to do it.

A: I did. It's very complicated.

Later, I am in another courtroom in Manhattan, one with a nameplate that reads HON. DEBORAH KAPLAN, PART SA, for 'substance abuse'. The judge sits with her palms clasped to a slender face and looks straight ahead.

Deborah Kaplan comes from an unlikely place where crime mixes with the neighbourhood air you breathe. Bensonhurst is quiet and substantial, and yet for so long the place was Fort Benning for the Mafia. The young watched and mimicked the regular infantry and foraged wherever they could. The house where she was raised is a

205

two-storey red brick with a basement, a stoop with seven steps and a small front porch. There is an American flag outside on the day I take a look. The house next door has an evergreen tree in front. There is a Dental Associates and a Chase bank on the corner. It is a solid neighbourhood house, from which Burt Kaplan left for a day's work selling clothing or to murder or for a couple of years in a federal prison. His parting was always the same as he walked out the front door: 'I'll be back.'

She came out of the State University at Albany, a big-league school, and St John's University Law School, which turned out Hugh Carey and Mario Cuomo, consecutive governors of New York. She was a clerk for Jerry Shargel, a highly intelligent defence lawyer. One of her father's own lawyers, Judd Burstein, was able to place her as a clerk for his mother, State Supreme Court Judge Bea Burstein, as substantial a name as you can get in New York judiciary and politics.

Deborah Kaplan knew how to go from there. She was president of the State Women's Bar Association and then ran for a civil-court judgeship out of the East Side political club, the Tilden Democratic Club.

> **Q:** At some point you learned that your daughter wanted to become a judge, didn't you?
>
> **A:** I was in prison, and my wife told me that my daughter was going to run for a judge, yes.
>
> **Q:** And it was pretty obvious, wasn't it, that if you came out and brought yourself a lot of attention, your daughter's chances of being elected a judge were zero?
>
> **A:** I don't know what you mean. I was doing twenty-seven years.

She has flowers on her high bench and a family photo in a silver frame. She has a mother, a husband and a son adopted from Russia.

In the quiet courtroom, a prisoner is brought from the detention pen, behind a door to her left. He wears a blue basketball jacket. A large man with a sheaf of papers, a Legal Aid lawyer, comes up to stand beside him.

A woman assistant district attorney says the man was arrested for the attempted theft of a computer printer from a Bronx appliance store.

The defendant mumbles to his lawyer, who says to the judge, 'He was passing the store, and he found the printer atop a parked car. He was walking it back into the store when the guard stopped him.'

The assistant district attorney says, 'He has himself going the wrong way. He wasn't going back into the store. He was walking out of it with the printer when the guard stopped him.'

The defendant protests. The judge looks through her papers. He had been in for a couple of days while they moved his work from the Bronx to her court. She gives him time served.

As he walks up the aisle, he stops and asks me for the subway fare home to the Bronx. All I have is a ten-dollar bill. I ask if he has change.

He shakes his head. The lawyer, a big rumpled man, comes rushing over. What am I doing to his client?

I show him the ten. 'Can you break it and I'll give him the car fare?'

The lawyer holds up his hands. He is unable to break a ten. He has no pocket change for his client either. He walks off. I tell the defendant that I am sorry, but I can't give him the whole ten. I have to get home, too.

He leaves. I concentrate on Deborah Kaplan. She stares straight down the aisle at me but gives nothing, no nod, no look to show that she knows why I am there. No, she has not answered the note I had sent earlier. She does not wish to talk.

TWENTY-TWO

Q: And you mentioned in 2004 that you did actually begin to cooperate: is that correct?

A: I was in jail nine straight years. I was on the lam two and a half years before it. In that period of time, I seen an awful lot of guys that I thought were stand-up guys go bad, turn and become informants.

As I told Steve Caracappa the night I left to go on the lam, I asked him if he could guarantee me that Louie would stand up, and Steve said, Yeah, I could do that.

And after nine years, I felt that they were going to be indicted by the state on this case, and I didn't think that they would stand up, and I was tired of going to jail by myself, and I would be at the defence table now, and Steve Caracappa and Louie Eppolito would be sitting up here.

Q: Did you plead guilty to a RICO conspiracy count?

A: Yes.

Q: As a result of that plea, what sentence, potential sentence, are you facing under that agreement?

A: Zero to life.

Q: Are you currently serving a sentence now for a previous case?

A: Yes.

Q: Can you please tell the jury, sir, what are your obligations under that agreement, as you understand them to be?

A: That I have to tell the truth about everything I know.

Q: Do you have to testify if you're called as a witness?

A: At any time?

Q: At any time. Do you have a choice about what cases you testify in?

A: No.

Q: Are you required to fully disclose all of your criminal activity?

A: Yes.

Q: And are you required not to commit any additional crimes? Either in prison or out of prison?

A: Yes.

Q: What is your understanding of the government's obligations under that agreement?

A: If I testify truthfully, the government will recommend certain things for me, four levels total downward departure in my sentencing. They would also write a 5K1 letter in this particular case and that they would write a Rule 35 to the judge on my previous case.

Q: The Rule 35, is that a sentencing-reduction letter?

A: It's a letter stating what cooperation I gave to the government and requesting the government to understand that I gave the cooperation.

Q: Is it your understanding that the government recommends to the court any particular sentence under that agreement?

A: No.

Q: What is your understanding of what those letters would consist of, the 5K letter and the Rule 35 letter?

A: They would state my cooperation in different cases.

Q: And if you testify falsely or give false information to the government or the agents, is the government still obligated to write you a 5K letter?

A: No.

Q: If you testify falsely or give false information to the government or the agents, is the government still obligated to write you a Rule 35 letter?

A: No. It is a letter given to informants, and you must tell the whole truth.

Q: Did the government agree to allow you to move for bail under your 5K case, this case?

A: Yes.

Q: And who decides whether you get bail or not?

A: The judge.

Q: And as you understand it, just yes or no, is the judge obligated to follow the government's recommendation in terms of bail?

A: No.

Q: As you understand it, is either judge, the Rule 35 judge or the 5K judge, obligated to reduce your sentence or to give you any particular sentence based upon the letter that is received from the government?

A: No.

Q: If the judge deciding your Rule 35 decides not to
give you a sentence reduction and the judge deciding
your 5K decides to give you no time in prison, how
much time in prison are you facing?

A: About thirteen or fourteen more years.

Q: If the judge – on the other hand, if the judge deciding
your Rule 35 decides to give you a sentence reduction
to time served and the judge deciding your 5K decides
to give you life in prison, how much time will you
serve?

A: Life in prison.

Q: And who is it that you understand that decides your
sentence? Is it the judge or the US Attorney's
office?

A: Decides my sentence?

Q: Yes.

A: The judge.

MR HENOCH: No further questions, Your Honour. Thank you.

Kaplan steps off the witness stand. A marshal holds a door. Kaplan
leaves as if he has not been here.

'Anybody want pound cake?' Bruce Cutler says. He has dessert and
coffee on the defence table. The jury is out.

In the corridor, Ms June Lowe, the court officer, dressed today
in brown, comes around the corner from the jury room. She has a
small smile as she brushes past people. She has a piece of paper in
her hand.

'Verdict,' she says.

She swings into the courtroom, causing those on benches in the
hallway to rise up and follow.

The defendants are at the table. The judge strides to the bench. The jury enters. June Lowe stands directly in front of the bench with several pages of verdict sheets. The jury forewoman is about fifteen feet away. She stands and the other jurors sit. She faces June Lowe, and June Lowe faces her, and the two of them take the breath out of the room.

June Lowe says, 'Racketeering Act One. Israel Greenwald Kidnapping. Conspiracy. Defendant Eppolito.'

This forewoman, whose name is hers and not of the record of this matter, who comes from a place you don't know, whose faith, if any, is hers, and who was brought here today by chance, stands and says in the same small voice we first heard during voir dire:

'Proved.'

'Defendant Caracappa,' June Lowe says.

'Proved,' the small voice says again.

Seventy times they say this in a courtroom that is still. There are no sighs of hopelessness, no rustles of satisfaction.

The voice grows smaller as the magnitude of what it is doing rises. This woman is destroying forever the evil she has been asked to judge.

When the last charge is read, the judge tells the jury thank you, you may go home, and they leave, and now he says immediately, 'Bail is revoked. The defendants are remanded. Marshals take charge.'

The word 'remanded' frightens Leah Greenwald, the widow of Jeweller Number Two. 'Does that mean he can go free?' she asks. The man next to her says, 'No. It means they put two locks on the cell door.'

A towering marshal moves up to Eppolito. Another goes to Caracappa. Others are around the room.

I'm a cop and I know what to do, Louie Eppolito says with his hands. He reaches under his jacket and pulls out his belt and throws it on the defence table. No guard has to tell him about prisoners hanging themselves. He is in a grey suit that has been stretched by a torso now as wide as a sidewalk. It is wrinkled from all the hours of writhing in a chair at the defence table. He takes off his gold-yellow tie and throws it on the desk. He takes the gold chain from around his neck and drops that. Then a watch, a ring, a wallet and still more items. His daughter, sitting behind him, holds out her hand, and he gives her the watch and chain. I know every step that a man takes when he has been convicted. I am Louie Eppolito, and I am a first-grade detective, a hero cop.

Down the table, Caracappa has his tie off without anybody noticing it. You cannot see what else he put on the table.

One kisses a daughter; one hugs a tearful lawyer. Caracappa, without tie, walks ahead of the marshal to the door to the detention pens. Behind him, Lou Eppolito swaggers, tieless and collar open to show a huge neck.

They disappear in mid-afternoon in Brooklyn through a door and into the perpetual darkness of their lives to come.

Somewhere astride his blue Schwinn, Nicky Guido calls out, 'One Adam-twelve.'

Later, in a cell at the Federal House of Detention several blocks away, the two cops decide that their lawyers were no good in that they had not won the case. Forget that the cops had failed to come up with one witness to refute a single solitary sentence of Burton Kaplan's crashing and thoroughly believable testimony. 'They refused to let me get up and testify for myself,' Eppolito says, claiming incompetent representation. He wants new lawyers and a new trial.

Weinstein sets 5 June for sentencing. When that day comes, he says, 'It is hard to visualise a more heinous offence.' He says the two cops had been convicted of 'the most serious series of crimes ever tried in this courthouse. There has been no doubt, and there is no doubt, that the murders and other crimes are proven without a reasonable doubt.' He says he was going to sentence them to life and million-dollar fines, but he cannot do this because of their appeal, which is based on the RICO statute of limitations problem that has hung over this trial since day one. Weinstein is not throwing away the law at the moment. Nor does it look like he will ever do so. He says he will give his decision on 30 June.

THE COURT: Does the defendant wish to make a statement?

EPPOLITO: Yes, sir.

THE COURT: I will hear you.

EPPOLITO: Your Honour, I have been a police officer for twenty-two and a half years. I know the feelings that every single family had here today. I handled as a detective many, many homicides, and I know how they feel from inside their guts. Sometimes I'm the one that goes to the house and knocks on the door and tells them there has been a death in the family. I don't know what I'm allowed to do or what I'm allowed to say. Of course, it comes from my heart. I would invite the Greenwalds, the Linos, the Hydells to come and visit me in jail, let me tell them the story. I was not allowed to do that. I had no opportunity to do that.

THE COURT: I don't want to hear that.

EPPOLITO: OK. If I was afforded the opportunity to talk to these families, if it was OK, if they wanted to sit with me and ask me and I could provide to them, I think I would prove to them I didn't hurt anybody ever. My first seventeen years as a police officer, I went to work with broken fingers, broken hands, stab wounds. I never missed a day's work. It is when I had my first heart attack I couldn't work. After I had my heart attack, I started writing, and I could find out I was able to write and tell a story. That's what I concentrated on. When I moved out of New York, it was not to move away from the people.

(Mr Gibbs stands.)

THE COURT: Marshal. Mr Marshal. Stop.

MR GIBBS: Remember me? Remember, Mr Eppolito?

THE COURT: Remove him.

Mr Barry Gibbs jumps out of the middle of the spectators, a large and loud shambles of a man. The judge is not terribly provoked. The marshals do not rush up to him so quickly. Gibbs is breaking all rules of courtroom behaviour. But he also has been frightfully wronged by this fat cop.

> **MR GIBBS:** I had a family, too. You remember what you did to my family? You don't remember what you did to my family and to me? Remember what you did to me? Me. Do you remember? You framed me. Do you remember what you did to me? Barry Gibbs. Do you remember? I had a family, too. You remember what you did to my family? You don't remember what you did to my family and to me? Remember what you did to me? Me. Do you remember?

Gibbs has come here from his single room in the Prince George Hotel, which takes the indigent and is in the dreary commercial blocks on the lesser streets of the East Side of Manhattan. This is far better than the prison cell Gibbs inhabited for nineteen years. He was there because Eppolito had threatened a witness into testifying falsely that Gibbs had strangled a prostitute. Now he has been released from prison, and his case is in the hands of Barry Scheck and Peter Neufeld, who run the Innocence Project in New York. Their record of using DNA to open cell doors for people wrongly convicted and put away for long sentences is astounding. They have freed some two hundred poor souls so far. If they don't get a Nobel Prize, it is a contempt of life that even Judge Weinstein cannot correct.

> (Mr Gibbs exits the courtroom.)

> **THE COURT:** I request that those present in court not repeat this demonstration. Proceed, sir.

> **EPPOLITO:** As far as Mr Gibbs was concerned, he also was afforded the same opportunity I was, and he went before a jury, and he had a very good attorney who fought for him. I never, ever

in my career interviewed the man who stated that I forced him to talk bad about Mr Gibbs, ever. That's what I can say about that. I never interviewed that man or that witness. Getting back to what I'm saying for today is, I have a family. I would feel the same way these people do. I could feel the hate and the sorrow. Your Honour, I've always felt that's why I became a cop. I had to live down my father. My father was a member of the Gambino crime family. I told people many, many times, it is like holding a child and saying to a child, I'm going to work hard. I'm going to give you the best education, I'm going to give you college and make sure you become a doctor or a lawyer and put him down. My father didn't do that to me. He told me, You better get a job and do what you're going to do. You're an Eppolito, you will not be able to get a liquor licence, a licence anywhere in the state, because of who I am. I was already crucified with the name before I had an opportunity.

I turned my back on organised crime so much, I just turned my back on it. I had no respect for them, I had no liking for them. I turned down every opportunity to speak to me.

My first fourteen years on the job, I worked in the Seventy-nine, the Seventy-seven, the Seventy-five, Twenty five Precinct in Harlem. I was never associated or around them. Yet when I first got in trouble, I asked them, I begged them, show me a picture of me with any organised crime families. Please, show me a photograph. Show me a phone tap with my name on it talking to somebody about anything about crime. And the one thing that I was so proud of as a human being, whether it is in jail or home or whether it is anywhere, that I have to go to my grave, is I was one hell of a cop. I tried my best on every case.

There were times where I used to go into the houses and tell people, I will work as hard to find out who took your baby's carriage as for who killed somebody. I never felt that I was going to get into a thing like this or being introduced to a piece of garbage in the street and thinking he is a nice person. Nobody had to – had the audacity or the nerve to approach me and ask me if I wanted to earn money. I worked hard, I had three children, married to the same lady all these years. I never, ever, ever did anything, ever, that I would have to embarrass my children. Yet in the last two years when this all broke, I was willing to go to the government, sit there and have them ask me any questions they could. I was willing to take my polygraph test. I took the so-called DNA test. Anything that was asked of me, I did. I just was not able to sit down and present a case, because I found it was so flawed to me, because I was a detective, I wasn't a guy who worked on a truck. I know how these things are.

I worked cases with the government, I worked cases with the state, I worked cases with the city. I have been before judges and I have said to them there is no reason for me to lie. I didn't need thirty thousand dollars to harm Mr Greenwald. I never heard Mr Greenwald's name in my life. When they mentioned it when we were incarcerated in Las Vegas, I said I never heard of a person like that, I never heard of the human being, I never heard of these times they said, Oh, you spoke to this guy. I never had access to them. I never had access to files or who it was.

When I heard this, I said to people, This is coming down on me because of who I am, who I was, not because of what I've done. I've always maintained my honesty, my integrity. I tried so hard. But I said to the government, Show me a piece of paper, a picture of me in a bar, in a club, show me. No, we don't have it. Where did I meet an organised-crime figure? Where was my phone? My phone was open, I was in the phone book. Never did any of these things.

When they lock onto something, like I did as a detective, it stays there. Selectively, they said what they want. It was selective, and I'll prove it to this court on a later date. It is all I have to say.

I apologise for having to speak for the first time until all this happened. I can hold my head up high. I never done any of this.

To Mrs Hydell, Otto Heidel's daughter, Mrs Lino and Mrs Greenwald, please call the judge, let you visit me. If I can't convince you I'm innocent, I will apologise. I didn't do any of these crimes at all.

Thank you.

THE COURT: Thank you.

Mr Caracappa.

DEFENDANT CARACAPPA: My lawyer will speak for me, Your Honour.

That was 5 June 2006. Jack B. Weinstein then went into his office and worked on a seventy-seven-page verdict, which he distributed on 30 June and the conclusion of which read:

> Defendants' motions for a judgment of acquittal pursuant to Federal Rule of Trial Procedure are granted as to the racketeering conspiracy charge and denied as to the narcotics charges. Although defendants' motions for a new trial pursuant to Federal Rule of Criminal Procedure 33 are denied, spillover prejudice from the dismissed racketeering charge requires retrial on both the money laundering and narcotics charges.
>
> If the Court of Appeals for the Second Circuit reinstates the jury verdict on the racketeering conspiracy charge, a new trial should be denied on all counts as to both defendants. For reasons announced on 5 June 2006, the sentence of defendant Eppolito will then be life on count one, 20 years on count two, 40 years on count three, and 40 years on count four, all to be served concurrently; five years of supervised release, a special assessment of 400 dollars and a fine of 1,000,000 dollars, with detailed conditions and terms as stated on the record. The sentence of defendant Caracappa will be: life on count one, 40 years on count three, and 40 years on count four, all to be served concurrently; five years of supervised release; a special assessment of 300 dollars and a fine of 1,000,000 dollars, with detailed conditions and terms as stated on the record.
>
> AS ORDERED
> JACK B. WEINSTEIN

As he said on that first day that they brought Burton Kaplan into his sealed courtroom to start the case, Weinstein believed that the government's RICO charge ran afoul of the statute of limitations. He still did at the end. Ms Lowe took the seventy-seven-page decision and handed it out to lawyers and news reporters. All the convictions for conspiracies to kill, to kidnap, to betray the citizens of the city – all were tossed out. Weinstein also had to allow new trials for money-laundering and narcotics charges. Immediately, the prosecution started the work of appealing the judge's ruling. At least many months could pass. Meanwhile, the Kings County district attorney's office is still waiting, waiting for the case to leave federal hands so they can prosecute the cops for James Hydell's murder.

Whatever happens while awaiting appeals and new trials and so on, the cops will be rotting in a prison cell. They will almost certainly do so until death.

There is one more matter to handle.

At 2.30 p.m. on 13 September 2006, Burt Kaplan strides through the door and into the courtroom. Somewhere they are playing his music. He doesn't look left, and he doesn't look right. He has on a dark suit and a red tie and a face full of determination. He goes right to a table and sits down. He is here to claim his end of the agreement. He ended a public horror. Now he wants to walk out of jail. Payday.

A lawyer sits with him. Next enter two assistant US Attorneys, Mitra Hormozi and Robert Henoch. Henoch is here from Fort Dix, where he has been recalled into the New Jersey National Guard as a lieutenant colonel.

Now in comes Federal District Court Judge Jack B. Weinstein in a double-breasted grey suit. He hadn't put on robes once in the month-long trial. He sits across from Kaplan with a large book of papers. Next to the judge is his assistant, June Lowe.

In a low voice, a conference voice, Weinstein says that on 13 January 1998, Burt had been sentenced to three hundred and twenty-four months in prison. He has served nine years. That equals one hundred and eight months out of three hundred and twenty-four. Which leaves a way to go.

Weinstein observes that Kaplan's testimony had been excruciatingly corroborated. What's more, he says that at Kaplan's behest, the murder of Virginia Robertson, killed in Brooklyn, was brought back. Eppolito had grabbed Barry Gibbs and framed him for the killing. Gibbs stood up in court and roared at Eppolito. The man committed no crime and yet served nineteen years in jail. Were it not for Kaplan, the agents never would have been able to obtain the warrant that let them into Eppolito's house in Las Vegas. There, among many things, they found, like cards face-up on the table, the papers that had put Gibbs away. The witness against Gibbs had been coerced by the Mafia cop. Thanks to Kaplan, Gibbs was free.

Weinstein then goes to his book on Kaplan's status under Rule 35, which dictates releases from prison. Weinstein reads the rule aloud about correcting errors. Subtitle B, within a year of sentencing, B2, and another initial, and then he looks at Henoch.

'You're relying on B2 A, information not known until a year or more,' Weinstein says. Henoch says yes. Weinstein reads, 'Prison assault case in 2004, Rule 35 not applicable without the Mexican... no reduction, an anomaly in the law that has serious complications in the law . . . The defendant has an astounding memory . . . He knows Eppolito's girl, wife, knife collection. The wife was a blonde now, a brunette then . . . The phone book . . . Santora phone slip in records of Peter Franzone . . .'

Then, as an aside, Weinstein says, 'The family is not here. They should be.' A stinging lesson for all in trouble in the future.

A lawyer for Kaplan says, 'The daughter was humiliated.'

'Nonsense,' Weinstein says. He asks Kaplan if he has anything to say.

So far, nobody has told Burt that he will go home. All they've done is mention numbers that seem to disqualify him. Now they want a last plea. They could be putting him back for ever. Kaplan tries the only thing he can trust: throw the truth right down the middle and see what happens.

'During this time, my only concern was selfish and [to] try not to get caught . . . I told the complete truth. I want to thank the agents and US Attorneys who proved I could be trusted.'

Weinstein goes right back to his book. 'Rule 35 C – a sentence more than one year from motion. Subassistance complies . . . Court has reduced sentence . . . 35 B4 not directly applicable . . . 5K . . . based on authority, time served.' Kaplan is having his freedom, the map of his new life, created as he sits.

Finally, Weinstein says, 'On the agreement on the RICO, bail is two million. The house valued at over five hundred thousand dollars. Abscond?'

Henoch says, 'No, sir. Bail is assured.'

Weinstein says, 'Bail granted.'

A man is out of prison.

Burt Kaplan's head drops on his chest. I am sitting behind his right shoulder, but his head is tilted to the left. I get up and move around so I can look directly at his face to see what emotion he displays.

His head is lowered only because he is signing papers. He is looking to his left because he is left-handed. His face is blank as he finishes signing.

He stands and says nothing and walks around the table and nods to nobody and looks at nobody and goes straight out the door.

INSIGHTS, INTERVIEWS AND MORE . . .

About the author

About the book

Read on

ABOUT THE AUTHOR

MEET JIMMY BRESLIN

Jimmy Breslin was born in Jamaica, Queens, on 17 October 1930 and began his newspaper career as a copy boy at the *Long Island Press* in 1948. He became a columnist for the legendary *New York Herald Tribune* in 1963, moving on to the *New York Post* in 1968. He was awarded the Pulitzer Prize for Distinguished Commentary in 1986, while a columnist for the *New York Daily News*. In 1988, he joined *Newsday*, where he is still a frequent contributor despite having officially retired in 2004. In addition to his recognition as a nationally syndicated columnist, Breslin also became a household name in 1969, when he ran for New York City councilman on the same ticket that featured Norman Mailer as the city's mayoral candidate, and in 1977, when serial killer David Berkowitz, known as Son of Sam, began corresponding with him. His bestselling and critically acclaimed books include a biography of Damon Runyon, *The Gang That Couldn't Shoot Straight*; *Can't Anybody Here Play This Game?*; *The Short Sweet Dream of Eduardo Gutiérrez*; several anthologies; and the memoir *I Want to Thank My Brain for Remembering Me*. He lives in New York City.

JIMMY BRESLIN:
IN THE NEWS AND IN HIS OWN WORDS

IN THE NEWS

'So many people do a good job of writing about this city that at any given moment there are hundreds of them at the big daily papers, scores of weeklies, magazines, and now Web sites, all hard at work, excavating and deciphering news. The best do it with heart, leaning into the story with the same determination as a late-inning relief pitcher. . . . For forty years, however, James Breslin has been the standout player in this league, bar none. Breslin himself will gladly tell you this.'

– Village Voice, 19 March 2002

'The thing about Jimmy Breslin, O.K., is he's a guy when he walked into a lounge on Queens Boulevard none of the wiseguys got uptight. We always thought he was one of us, O.K.? He could have a cocktail at the bar, O.K., and wasn't looking to zap you. He brings me up to date on New York City and I tell him all the best-kept secrets in Las Vegas. You know they say what happens in Vegas stays in Vegas? Well, what happens in Vegas gets to Jimmy Breslin.'

*– Sal Reale, a former associate of the Gambino family,
New York Times*, 20 January 2008

'He stands in the foreground: the tough and tender journalist, cynical but sentient, a flowery writer but also a gifted one. He dabbles among clichés and comes up with discoveries. At its best his work has the impact of a different art: that of Daumier and Rowlandson.'

– Newsday, 15 September 1996

'Jimmy Breslin's colleagues at the old *New York Herald Tribune* used to wonder how much of his Runyonesque column was fiction. The question was settled with the suggestion that Jimmy did not write fiction because he had enough trouble making up the truth. That, in part, was how the New Journalism was born. From barroom, cloakroom and police station Breslin cut slices of life in which big guys squeezed little guys; people who read too many books didn't know what they were talking about; and politicians were vain, greedy and corrupt – except Bobby Kennedy, who got shot as Breslin watched. Nobody wrote a better eyewitness piece about the assassination.'

– *Time*, 14 June 1982

'Mr. Breslin's bona fides as a newspaperman need no introduction: there was the early stint as a copy boy at the *Long Island Press*; triumphant sojourns at the *New York Herald Tribune* and the *Daily News*; the brutal beating at the hands of a Lucchese family gangster who didn't much care for an article he once wrote; and, of course, the chilling receipt of a loony letter from David Berkowitz, the serial killer known as Son of Sam. . . . And with a past like that, it would perhaps be excusable if Mr. Breslin simply churned out pieces from the time capsule and sat back on his journalistic laurels. . . . [H]e remains quite busy – as a crank, a scold, a public nuisance, a curmudgeon of the foulmouthed Irish mold, who has made a cottage industry out of keeping alive the grit, vitality and maverick spirit of New York's phone-booth-and-fedora days.'

– *New York Times*, 20 January 2008

'Outrageously, he claims to have devised the art of covering a big story by going somewhere the rest of the pack hadn't thought of. His interview with an Arlington Cemetery gravedigger on the day of John F. Kennedy's funeral is still taught in journalism schools, he writes. Editors, he writes, are still telling young reporters: "Go find the gravedigger."'

– *Newsday*, 15 September 1996

'In 1977, Jimmy Breslin was at the top of his game. . . . Breslin turned out gritty, intimate columns, bursting with staccato prose and human voices and Irish melancholy. In person, he was a tangle of contradictions: playful, blustery, vainglorious, always ready with an insult. Given his celebrity status, it wasn't entirely surprising that Breslin himself became a dramatic character in the "Son of Sam" case: In the same column in which he printed excerpts from the Berkowitz letter, Breslin pleaded: "The only way for the killer to leave this special torment is to give himself up to me, if he trusts me, or to the police."'

– Columbia Journalism Review,
November–December 2001

'Jimmy Breslin may not be the world's last passionate man, but you have the feeling that he's one of a group so small it could convene at a table in the Automat – and it was never that large a group to begin with. . . . Breslin, who won a Pulitzer Prize not long ago for his three-a-week columns in the *New York Daily News*, is large, profane, restless, enthusiastic and urgent. You can't imagine him being indifferent about anything – from breakfast eggs to the state of the New York Police Department or the world.'

– Los Angeles Times, 7 June 1986

'Much as he has done throughout that career, Mr. Breslin rises early each day, at six a.m., first to swim at the Reebok gym near his apartment, then to read the city's daily papers, then finally to write. It is a *modus vivendi* much helped by the fact that, in the early 1980s, he gave up his Olympic bouts of drinking, following, he claims, an epic bender with Senator Daniel Patrick Moynihan resulting in a hangover of such destructive force that he was still crippled after three days.'

– New York Times, 20 January 2008

IN HIS OWN WORDS

On writing

'Rage is the only quality which has kept me, or anybody I have ever studied, writing columns for newspapers.'

– The Times, 9 May 1990

'It's worse than heroin. . . . Oh. It's awful. It's like you get mad at the world when nothing big happens the day before. . . . I mean, you look, what did they do? There's nothing going on. Didn't somebody get shot or a politician do something? Nothing.'

– Sunday Morning, CBS, 9 March 2008

'It is an Irish thing to be with the underdog. My mother was a social worker, and she had a temper about things. And I come out of the old days in the newspapers when there was smoke and noise and . . . yelling in the city room, there was excitement and all words for a newspaper are a product of nervous excitement, I say. Today, it's different. It's calm, it's cool, you've got a computer, the people aren't out in bars, they're not smoking, they're very healthy, very smart, and very boring.'

– Today, NBC, 3 July 2002

'You still walk (to gather news), you climb stairs and all the stories are at the top of the stairs. You get into trouble when you get there using an elevator. They [reporters] don't climb the stairs anymore, they don't understand the shoe-leather, they don't teach that in their high-class schools. They are highly trained people who sit in their offices and write term papers. They won't sully themselves going to a greasy housing project or stand out in the rain for a few hours.'

– Editor & Publisher, 9 June 2003

'It's the greatest thing in the world [the life of a reporter]. Anybody who doesn't go into it is a sucker. . . . The daily surprises of news keep you from getting sick. I went 50 years, I never had a cold.'

– *Sunday Morning*, CBS, 9 March 2008

'I work at home and I got three newspaper columns a week. That's the day job. I'm doing this book and we have – my wife and I, between us, have nine kids. . . . So I'm trying to finish the book and worry about a column, and one of her daughters comes in with three kids from the suburbs and just puts them in the door. . . . She shuts the door and runs, and I got three kids, grandchildren, which the average grandparent and grandchild can stay together without venom for about 6.5 minutes. After that, everybody hates each other. They do. So I'm there and these kids, they don't talk to me. They don't like me enough to talk to me, and I don't like them. But at any rate, they . . . walk over to the television and the next thing, I turn around, they got *Thumbelina* on. They just put it on. They don't know what to do. So I said, "Take that thing off." They wouldn't. So I get it out. And we had a war and it was traumatic. I couldn't get any work done that day.'

– *Today*, NBC, 3 July 2002

'Don't trust a brilliant idea unless it survives the hangover.'

– *Nation's Restaurant News*, 4 February 2002

On immigration

'I had to go out to the desert to see for myself where they are putting up this ridiculous fence (along the U.S.–Mexico border). Then I came back to New York, and while I was sitting in a coffee shop I learned all I needed from an immigrant who was working the counter. Who wouldn't want these people in the country? A cup of coffee would cost 10 bucks. If you don't let them in, who will do all the dirty work? Not white people. If the government shuts down the border and kicks these people out, there won't be one hotel chambermaid from New York to San Francisco.'

– Playboy, 1 January 2007

On churchgoing

'I stopped when I made a pronouncement that [New York cardinal Edward] Egan ought to get thrown out, that I'd have nothing more to do with him. I really believe the hierarchy of the Catholic Church in America are pimps, and the rank-and-file are pedophiles. Deny it if you can. Don't tell me it's the work of only a few.'

– Publishers Weekly, 28 June 2004

On the Mob

'You can get money without working – I'm going to get a Mercedes car, I'm going to get a big pinky ring, and I'm going to get a woman that doesn't know how to behave and we're going to go out big Tuesday night. You want me to go back to school and then go to work some place, in a factory or work in some manual labor for what, $10 an hour? As opposed to what, I get 5,000? Get out of here.'

– Sunday Morning, CBS, 9 March 2008

'Normally, you don't need a gangster with a high IQ. It doesn't take any brains – I mean, to send a guy across the street for cigars would be hard on them sometimes. No, a lot of them can't read and write.'

– Tell Me More,
National Public Radio, 4 March 2008

On not watching *The Sopranos*

'I had a little trouble with it because it was based in the suburbs, and I don't recognize anything that doesn't have an el [subway] running through it.'

– Tell Me More,
National Public Radio, 4 March 2008

On Norman Mailer

'This was a massive worker. I mean, in honest, essentially, he never stopped working. Now and then, we'd drift out into the night and there'd be something that happened, got busted and you'd wind up with headlines and the shrieks. But essentially, he was a working man. When you mention Mailer to me, I think of Van Gogh's work boots.'

– Weekend Edition,
National Public Radio, 10 November 2007

On politics

'All political power is primarily an illusion. . . . Illusion. Mirrors and blue smoke, beautiful blue smoke rolling over the surface of highly polished mirrors, first a thin veil of blue smoke, then a thick cloud that suddenly dissolves into wisps of blue smoke, the mirrors catching it all, bouncing it back and forth.'

*– from How the Good Guys Finally Won:
Notes from an Impeachment Summer* (1975)

On beating the bottle

'When you stop drinking, you have to deal with this marvelous personality that started you drinking in the first place.' – from *Table Money*, 1986

INK-STAINED KVETCH

JIMMY BRESLIN

BORIS KACHKA INTERVIEWED JIMMY BRESLIN FOR NEW YORK MAGAZINE, 4 FEBRUARY 2008.

As the old columnists die out, Jimmy Breslin (whose style is equal parts Dickens and Yogi Berra) keeps pressing on. His new book, *The Mafia Rat*, tells the story of the 'Mafia cops' trial from the sort of side view he made famous when he interviewed JFK's grave-digger in 1963. It focuses on Burt Kaplan, the guy who spilled the beans. Breslin talked to Boris Kachka, with helpful interjections from his wife, former councilwoman Ronnie Eldridge.

So what makes a rat, like the one in the book, a good rat?

A good rat gets his name on the cover of a book. The publisher asked me to do a book on these Mafia cops. But I spoke to them and I became disinterested immediately. Then the door opened in the courtroom and in walked Kaplan. And they say, 'Are you in the Mafia?' and he says, 'No, I can't be. I'm Jewish.' The first thing that came to my mind was Dostoyevsky, looking at him.

You lament the death of the Mafia mainly because it deprives you of characters.

Well, who would you rather have? These animals in this book, or these hedge-fund operators? Who contributes the most to the electricity of the day in New York? They ought to let the Mafia shoot the hedge-fund people.

You called the election for Kerry on the last day of your Newsday column in 2004. Who are you calling it for this time?

We'll see, but I'm voting for Obama. Put the two of them up there and you listen to her. Then listen to him. If you're sick, you'll vote for her.

Whom do you blame for all the papers declining in circulation?

YouFace, these things, everybody seems to be looking at them. But newspapers are so boring. How can you read a newspaper that starts with a 51-word lead sentence? They're trying to prove they went to college.

And what do you think of today's columnists?

Jonathan Alter, he's a nice fellow. Brooks, worst I ever read in print. And the other guy, Kristol. He should be arrested if caught writing a postcard. Wolfey – Tom Wolfe – called the father [Irving Kristol] Irving Statistics. But that's when people could turn phrases.

Do you read any blogs?

I'm disinterested. RONNIE ELDRIDGE: [*In background*] You won't learn about them! JIMMY BRESLIN: They don't even go in barrooms. It's opinions written from the kitchen table!

Is that your wife arguing with you?

Yes. [*To Eldridge*] He wants to know why you're interrupting. R.E.: Because I always have to tell you what to do!

Okay, so do you use a computer now?

I had the last typewriter in New York. Now I use a computer, but it's cost me more time than hangovers. It skips, it misses, it sputters. R.E.: Can I just tell him . . . J.B.: Why?! He's trying to write a Q&A now! R.E.: [*Wrenching phone away*] He doesn't know anything about the computer, and he won't learn because he says he's not a mechanic. So it gets worse every day. Sorry! [*Gives phone back.*]

But isn't a computer faster, really?

Yeah, until the fucking thing takes a high dive.

By Boris Kachka.
Reprinted with permission of New York *magazine.*

READ ON

AUTHOR'S PICKS

BRESLIN'S FAVOURITES

The Grapes of Wrath by John Steinbeck
The Last Angry Man by Gerald Green
Boss by Mike Royko
Dreaming in Cuban by Cristina Garcia
The Shipping News by Annie Proulx
Final Payments by Mary Gordon
The Gambler by Fyodor Dostoyevsky
Crime and Punishment by Fyodor Dostoyevsky
The Adventures of Tom Sawyer by Mark Twain
The Adventures of Huckleberry Finn by Mark Twain
Light in August by William Faulkner
The Sun Also Rises by Ernest Hemingway
Run to Daylight! by Vince Lombardi with W. C. Heinz
Love in the Time of Cholera by Gabriel García Márquez
Essays by Michel de Montaigne
Short Stories of Honoré de Balzac by Honoré de Balzac
The Importance of Being Earnest by Oscar Wilde
This Was Racing by Joe H. Palmer
The Briar Patch: The Trial of Panther 21 by Murray Kempton